THE ALCHEMY OF STORIES

Essays on Literature and Life

Edited by
Monika Lee and Clara Sebben

OPEN
BOOKS
ACADEMIC

Published by Open Books Academic

Interior design by Siva Ram Maganti

Cover image © Shutterstock AI Generator
shutterstock.com/g/ai-image-generator

Contents

Acknowledgements

We would like to acknowledge Western University's Office of the Dean of Arts and Humanities, the Department of English and Writing Studies, and the Smallman Fund for generous support of this project. We thank our talented, patient, and inspirational authors for sharing their stories with us. We wish to thank our families, especially Brian, Anna, Natasha, and Bonnie; Kim, Scott, and Casper. Thank you to Open Books Press, to Kelly and David, for their work and commitment to the project. We express our deep gratitude for Brescia University College, its students and alumnae, the School of Humanities and Department of English, where most of our writers once studied or taught, a community in which stories worked their alchemical magic and literature thrived.

Introduction

In the stillness of the COVID-19 lockdown, overextended workers and harried students found solace in reconnecting with books. Canadian book sales skyrocketed,[1] and literary forums sprang up on nearly every existing digital app, including the explosively popular BookTok, while the culture of reading continues to sweep through libraries, curls up in coffee shops, and clings to the corners of our daily commutes.[2] Literature is resilient and adaptable. It endures because it transforms. And, thanks to our reading, so do we.

Recent years have seen a resurgence of scholastic and public interest in the phenomenology, neurobiology, and sociology of reading.[3] Reconsidering human interaction with the written word, cognitive scientists, literacy scholars, and enthusiastic bookworms alike are

---

1. From 2020 to 2022, operating revenue for Canadian book publishers rose 8.3%: the largest comparable increase since 2014. ("The Resurgence of Readers: Bookworms are on the Rise." *Statistics Canada*, 2024).

2. In a 2020 BookNet Canada survey, part of a multi-year study entitled *Borrow, Buy, Read: Library Use and Book Buying in Canada*, 76% of respondents indicated that they read for enjoyment – a significant increase from the 59% who reported reading for pleasure in 2019. (Hirschberg, Shim. "Canadian Readers in 2020." *BookNet Canada*, 2020).

3. Recent publications like *The Science of Reading: Information, Media and Mind in Modern America* by Adrian Johns (2023), *Reader Come Home: The Reading Brain in a Digital World* by Maryanne Wolf (2018), *The Reading Cure: How Books Restored My Appetite* by Laura Freeman (2017) and *The Reading Mind: A Cognitive Approach to Understanding How the Mind Reads* by Daniel T. Willingham (2017) underscore this renewed multidisciplinary interest in the subject of reading.

posing provocative questions: What happens in our brains and bodies during immersive reading? What factors account for variations in the ways individuals register written text? Do our unique worldviews structure our reading experiences or vice versa?

Blending empirical inquiry and humanistic introspection in its methodology, *The Alchemy of Stories* positions itself at a critical juncture in these dialogues. Together, the selected essays explore what it means to "lose oneself" in a book and how such an ego dissolution paves the way for the reconstruction of personal identity. Moreover, the anthology makes a forceful argument for the enduring value of literature classes amid controversies surrounding declining Arts and Humanities enrolments, a phenomenon Nathan Heller has contentiously termed the "end of the English major."[4] Ironically, Heller's tagline has breathed new life into critical conversations surrounding the importance of English, Writing, and Creativity courses. Brimming with first-hand evidence that imaginative literature constellates identities and perspectives, *The Alchemy of Stories* will ride and sustain the momentum of a contemporary reading-culture renaissance.

For the past thirty-eight years, Monika has shared her love of stories with students, Canadian authors, and work colleagues from many nationalities, ethnicities, religions, ages, gender identities, sexual orientations, socio-economic groups, and backgrounds. She quickly lost count of students' epiphanic anecdotes and crazed fandoms, from which she concludes that to readers, to everyone really, the verbal arts are necessary, far more so than our contemporary cultures realize or acknowledge. As she likes telling her students, poetry and storytelling will outlive the stock market and the internet, because they have existed in every culture on earth and in every historical age. Like other art forms, they'll change radically over time, but they will disappear

---

4. Heller, Nathan. "The End of the English Major." *The New Yorker*, February 27, 2023.

only when humans disappear. Let's hope that the study of literary art also endures, because it's imperative that we attempt to know and understand why people are compelled to create it, and why all cultures on earth in every epoch require it.

Now that the university study of English has morphed from respectable to unrespectable, there are many apologists out there defending literary study to the naysayers. The time is ripe to tell one true but neglected story of why literature matters. Like Monika's former teacher Northrop Frey, in the word "literature" we do not distinguish between canonical and popular writing. Any literary text, whether Young Adult fiction, children's stories, pulp fiction, a medieval play, or the Bible, can be life changing. We would go so far as to say that every creative work we read, like a pebble in a pond, alters the pool of our minds, the lake of our lives, and the sea of the world in small ways, but this collection of essays addresses those more obvious inspirational moments which resurrect and recreate us, forming and framing ourselves in the world, and transforming who we are.

Great writing comes directly from great reading. Francine Prose's *Reading Like A Writer* expresses it well when she observes that novels and stories seemed to her "revelations: wells of beauty and pleasure that were also textbooks: private lessons in the art of fiction." Although it's true that reading books will improve one's I.Q., lead to better writing, assist critical thinking, and help a person become productively employed, the deeper reason for reading fiction is that it makes us better informed, more thoughtful, and more creative people. This book bears witness to how moved, changed, and sometimes shattered people are by their reading. We have heard countless anecdotes about love affairs with poetry or prose, with Jane Austen and Bram Stoker, with J.R.R. Tolkien and C.S. Lewis, with T.S. Eliot and Emily Dickinson, with our language and its myriad writers. These stories are individual, riveting, and provocative, whether about the student whose entire family opposes their major in English and refuses to fund anything but Business or STEM courses, and then that student takes out loans and works more than 20 hours a week, just so that they can read more Virginia Woolf, or about the student who was turned on to J.K. Rowling in childhood, cried herself to sleep at night because she couldn't attend Hogwarts, and is now an animal rights activist partly because of Hagrid but also for Dobby's sake; what we have noticed time and again is that the changes go deep. Literature re-made students and their lives, so they enrolled in English courses and degrees because they long for more transfigurations. They hunger for a rich inner life with all its bounty: self actualization, individuation, imagination, compassion for others, mental travel, aesthetic appreciation, contextualization, social cohesion, political understanding, ethical context, social justice, and maturation. Yes, books of imaginative writing can provide all these, and, unlike stocks and real estate, as we age, their value increases and never diminishes. In old age, professions disappear, friends die, the body falters, mobility suffers, but books remain loyal and steadfast friends, sharing their wealth generously, confirming the ongoing vibrancy of the human imagination, validating our existential struggles and spiritual longings, reaffirming our common humanity.

In a "Senior Seminar in Creativity," Monika experimented and had fun, as she taught and learned from a very lively group of eight students. They dressed up as their favourite literary characters and held a potluck in which they made a group painting and a collaborative soup which tasted like road tar. The question the course asked them was "What is creativity?" They wrote stories and poems, but the final assignment was to write a creative essay on a favourite literary text, like those in the course text, *Light the Dark* edited by Joe Fassler. A colleague suggested that they would make an excellent book. Monika hesitated. Of course, people would want to read the essays by Stephen King and Amy Tan, but why would anyone want to read a collection of essays by other aspiring writers? No sooner had she asked herself the question than she heard an answer which sprang excitedly from her unconscious: "because your students' journeys in and through their reading are universal among readers of fiction." All readers experience these transformative moments, and most serious readers also try their hands at creative writing, however briefly. A small ember was fanned and turned into flame by the thought of how many people's unspoken intimate experiences with reading could be fueled and corroborated.

A handful of substantially revised creative student essays (only four of our total 40) provided the kernel of a project which took on a life of its own, as creative writers and academics expressed interest in making contributions. Vanessa Brown is an award-winning author who has penned a Canadian bestseller, Sarah Pesce is the CEO of Lopt and Croft, an editorial agency which specializes in romance fiction, Joel Faflak, a member of the Royal Society, has authored and co-edited numerous books and essays, and won multiple awards on topics ranging from literature to psychology, and Scotty Olsen was accepted into Audible's prestigious Indigenous Writers' Circle. Many of our contributors are published authors, several are doctoral students or academics, and a few are graduates from MFA programmes. What they have in common is a love of reading and a talent for writing. Most of them noted how hard it was to select a single story when they have been shaped and changed by so many literary texts, when they love so many different authors. We sympathize with this dilemma. Almost every day of our lives, some passage of what we're reading arrests us with its power and beauty so as to shake our preconceptions and enlarge our perspective on the world. We have learned that such experiences, as uncanny and mysterious as they can feel, are authentic, powerful, and common as dust.

The book is divided into eight sections, each organized around a shared theme. In the inaugural section, "Hope," beloved books fan the flames of possibility and illuminate new ways of living. Jaya Sinha's essay about John Knowles and garbage trucks challenges notions of hope as an "easy thing, like picking out what to wear" and reframes it as a succession of raw, ungraspable eruptions of emotional clarity: "wild, directionless, completely out of your control." The section entitled "Freedom" features narratives which have broken readers' chains and harnessed emancipation. Carling Dekay, reading Mary Shelley's *Frankenstein*, moves from the shadows of repressive heteronormativity to queer visibility. The "Enchantment" section shows how literature casts spells which captivate and change us. Anna Lee-Diemert's lyrical essay "Trees" lulls us into a "dreamish wakefulness" where certainties dissolve, while she explores the nature of belief and questions the primacy of empirical evidence. In "Introspection," our writers unravel the tangled threads of creative consciousness and discover that "there is power in looking inwards." Musician-poet Matthew Rooney re-examines the epistemological foundations of his artistry, as he discovers through Elizabeth Bishop that knowledge is not static but oceanic: "historical, flowing, and flown." Literature becomes a compass and a map in the "Discovery" section, as readers like Carrie Kieswetter derive a sense of direction from their literary muses. Recounting how the words of Rick Riordan have charted the course of her creative career, Kieswetter embraces *The Lightning Thief* as a guiding meridian: "I will follow it wherever it takes me." In the section entitled "Healing," readers uncover the therapeutic properties of the creative written word. Shaped by the consolatory prose of Romain Gary, Catherine Courteau's "gentle and gradual exploration of death" nudges her towards a career in palliative medicine and helps her process a tragic childhood loss. The "Acceptance" section demonstrates how literature empowers us to embrace inevitabilities with serenity and grace. In Anita Diamant's *The Red Tent*, Kaatje Kempe finds permission to abandon her restless pursuit of existential meaning and bask in "the bliss of insignificance." The collection concludes with essays on "Resistance" which emphasize the role of literary engagement in promoting defiance and dissent. Audrey Thomas's *Mrs. Blood* emboldens Heather McCardell to challenge medical misogyny, while Frank McCourt's *Angela's Ashes* prompts Scotty Olsen to pen a memoir about his navigation of Canada's education system as an Indigenous teenager.

The bean counters, pragmatists, and gatekeepers who incessantly question the value of fiction are, sadly, the uninitiated, and this book does not intend to try to convince them of anything. Rather, this book unabashedly preaches to the choir, since bookworms understand what P.B. Shelley wrote long ago, that "poets," by which he meant all artists in all genres, are "the unacknowledged legislators of the world." Legislation happens only when the needle of public conscience moves first, and those changes in social opinion are begotten and fostered by art.

Readers are pilgrims. What a privilege it has been to travel on a journey through the world of words in the presence of other pilgrims. Sometimes, we stop and share a story, a meal, a passion, or a nod of recognition. One way to conceive of this anthology is as a collection of shared moments, because one thing our contributors have in common is not just their love of specific stories, authors, and passages, but also their profound sense of having been metamorphosed by their encounters with imaginative writing. We invite you to read this compendium of epiphanies as part of an interactive journey, one that can remind you of the narrative trajectory of your life. Moreover, the narrative arcs of your life intersect with broader historical, political, religious, and cultural trends in ways which shape and determine our whole world. *The Alchemy of Stories* is also a book about pedagogy, in the sense that great teaching comes from great content. Pedagogically speaking, students are teachers, and the learning process is a co-creation of the highest order, and this book is an ode in celebration of that creative process. May your lives' journeys be rich with story, metaphor, irony, humour, beauty, joy, freedom, adventure, and love, all of which exist in the imaginative Word.

I – HOPE

There Will Be Time

Clara Sebben

But as if a magic lantern threw the nerves in patterns on a screen:
Would it have been worthwhile
If one, settling a pillow or throwing off a shawl,
And turning toward the window, should say:
> *That is not it at all,*
> *That is not what I meant, at all.*

(*The Love Song of J. Alfred Prufrock* by T.S. Eliot)

When I was in the fourth grade, I developed a sudden stutter. Since I'd always been a chatty kid, my parents considered my speech impediment an emergency, and they hired a therapist to lead me through remedial exercises twice a week. She was lovely, all silver hair and grandmotherly scarves, but despite the stickers and animal-shaped erasers with which she bought my participation, I dreaded missing afternoon recess to act out fabricated dialogues and practice set phrases. On a day I was feeling particularly jaded, I remember asking her *why* I had to fix my stutter: couldn't people take an extra moment or two to listen?

The Love Song of J. Alfred Prufrock poses a similar question, and perhaps that's why the poem stirred me the way it did. It spoke to my exasperated fourth-grade self, someone I'd nearly forgotten. I was in my first-year dorm room the evening when, surrounded by textbooks, notes, and half-empty mugs of tea, I stepped into Prufrock's mazy world. Well, not immediately. First, tired and on edge, I scanned the text, a required reading for the next morning's class. I resisted the poem's pull because I was reading it incorrectly. My agenda was to extract some tidy allegory or well-defined message to discuss on an exam, and I'm ashamed to say that I was looking at Prufrock the way rushed adults once looked at me — with eyes that said *spit it out*.

But then I came across the line, "It's impossible to say just what I mean!" and, realizing the poem was not going to serve me a thesis on a silver platter, I renounced my original plan. Prufrock seemed to tell me to forget themes and symbols. He asked me to abandon the clock and the need to prove something. Once I stopped rushing to make sense of Prufrock's words, I yielded to his pull and entered his world. My second read-through was a vastly different experience. I no longer felt irritated at his half-deserted thoughts; instead, I felt relieved, for I didn't want ideas. What mattered to me then was not knowing his "overwhelming question" but feeling the deeply human pain of an inquiry burning inside of you, one you cannot release for lack of adequate words or lack of patient ears.

The hard truth I learned as a young stutterer was that no one had time for me to stumble over words, but *Prufrock* substantiates something I've always suspected: that great, authentic art transpires when we remove the imperative to be prompt. We value concision and efficiency in our day-to-day communications, and those are wonderful, productive qualities. But we often focus on them at the expense of thoughtfulness — how can we search our inner lexicons for the perfect sequence of words to represent some burning question, doubt, or hunch when someone is waiting with a tapping foot? It's an understatement to say that Prufrock is not a succinct speaker. All his probing and meandering take him nowhere, and he never finds the words to reveal that all-consuming question. Yet, until "human voices" wake him at the end of the poem, nobody cuts him off, nobody tells him to "get to the point," and nobody asks him to try out prepackaged expressions that might approximate his ineffable question. Maybe that's because this poem stops time. The opening line, "let us go, then, you and I," takes our hands and drags us into some indeterminate place devoid of urgency. "And indeed there will be time," Prufrock repeats. The "and indeed" is perfectly unnecessary, and it punctuates his statement as if to say, "this is a world with time for superfluity."

With its insistence on endless stores of time, the poem grants us permission to fumble for words. More importantly, it invites us not to hide this fumbling as part of some backstage process to be purged from the final draft. *Prufrock* asks us to resist making writing seem effortless — to leave our snags and hitches on the page and to make time for stutters. My favourite poems and books are the ones that represent the moment of their production. Reading these texts is like being inside a mind at work, arranging and rearranging phrases in real time. These works fumble and play a little, they might grope around for words, and no matter how many times we read them, they are always being composed gradually before our eyes. When writers make room for traces of the creative process, when they capture a moment of messy, uncensored thought, that's how they transcend time. There's a magical sense of contact between writer and reader as the former threads together words on the page and the latter pieces them together in their mind. It's a moment of shared vulnerability, and that allows a work to be reborn with each reading. It gives a text infinite lives.

For me, that mystical moment of contact happens here:

> But as if a magic lantern threw the nerves in patterns on a screen:
> Would it have been worthwhile
> If one, settling a pillow or throwing off a shawl,
> And turning toward the window, should say:
> >   "That is not it at all,
> >   That is not what I meant, at all."

The passage is muddy and perplexing, like tuning into the second half of a movie after missing the exposition. Would *what* have been worthwhile? *What* is not it at all? As I ask these questions, I feel T.S. Eliot grappling with them too, while Prufrock shrugs his shoulders. And I feel the poem's objective buried in that startling image, "as if a magic lantern threw the nerves in patterns on a screen": T.S. Eliot throws the nerves in patterns on the page, free from the constraints of clarity and efficiency and concision. To me, this passage is a window opening onto the scene of *Prufrock*'s inception. I can see his maker tossing pure emotion in the air and allowing it to fall into stanzas, like a painter flicking colour onto a blank canvas. This is why I read: to be transported across the borders of my own mind.

There's fear in this passage — a deep fear of being misunderstood. I face this fear every time I write. That's why I spend plenty of time lining up words and seeing how they look and sound and feel beside one another. I'll replace and rearrange until I find the lineup that best captures the thought or feeling I'd like to convey. But there's no perfect, foolproof arrangement, because words are fundamentally inadequate. And it's so painful when we come up against the limitations of language: when thrilling ideas, ones we ache to release, shrink in the light of day. The mere eight monosyllables of the line, "That is not what I meant at all," manage to capture the resigned shame of having a keen sentiment deflated in the attempt to express it.

I felt a shade of this disappointment when I shared the poem with my dad. He's a man of few words, but we have a quiet sort of connection. I saw him in Eliot's poem, and I wanted it to fill some of the silence between us. He liked it well enough, but it clearly didn't rattle him the way it rattled me. The poem didn't give him an unprecedented sense of companionship and consolation, nor did it make him see himself in a new light. That was when I saw first-hand how awful it is that words affect us so variously. I might read a passage that changed your life without feeling a thing, and you might scarcely notice a sentence that punched me in the gut. It's the supreme difficulty of not just writing but relating to anyone at all.

We all fear being misunderstood, and we enact little performances to protect ourselves. When we are most honest, we adopt airs of sarcasm or self-deprecation. We know we won't be wholly understood, so we diminish our own ideas and sentiments before they can be reduced by another person's inevitably imperfect understanding. Prufrock, too, engages in this sort of pre-emptive self-mockery. But what I love about this poem is that it does not mock or condemn our silly self-defensive manoeuvres. T.S. Eliot finds art — a *love song* — in the clumsy ways we struggle to express ourselves against all odds of success.

The Love Song of J. Alfred Prufrock seems to follow me, as though it knows I need to re-experience it now and then. In my second-year Poetics class, for instance, it appeared on the syllabus at the tail end of Modernism day. We hadn't arrived at T.S. Eliot by the time our professor dismissed us, and, as we were putting on our coats, someone asked, "What about *Prufrock*?" At 9:30 pm that snowy Wednesday, everyone stopped for eight minutes or so while our professor read the poem aloud. Given that we'd all encountered the text in previous courses, this break from our busy lives was perfectly unnecessary — some might say a "waste of time." But with that opening tug on the sleeve, everyone in the room seemed to forget half-zipped backpacks, the drive home, and the next day's obligations. There was a powerful, nearly sacred sense of shared emotion as we moved through the poem's meandering paths. Class was over, but there was time. We *made* time, and, thanks to *Prufrock*, I think we always will.

the soapdish on the sink

Nathan TeBokkel

In Kurt Vonnegut's *God Bless You, Mr. Rosewater, or Pearls Before Swine*, there's a little by-the-way still life of Fred and Caroline Rosewater's kitchen in Rhode Island. Fred's a depressed life insurance salesman who has been persuaded by a lawyer into scamming his relative Eliot, a millionaire, out of some cash. The book ends with Eliot giving Fred $100,000 and then adopting everyone in town, so they all have more claim to the rest of his fortune than Fred does. Fit for an electric chair and featuring a dried-up philodendron, the kitchen is lifeless except for the dirty hint that lies in the soapdish on the sink. This ball of soap, made from wetted, pressed-together bits of other bars, is the motley product of what the narrator calls Caroline's only art, learned from her mother, brought to her marriage.

I've been turning Vonnegut's words over in my mind the way Caroline might soften bits of soap before sticking them together. I've turned them over so many times I've made quite a lather. Since starting this essay, I've turned them over so often that lather might be all that's left. If nothing else, it might feel ticklish and smell refreshing. That would be okay by me. So it goes. But of all the unforgettable, irreverent sentences Vonnegut penned, why do I keep coming back to this part of the novel?

If the larger story is an improbable, compassionate jaunt, this vignette is bleak. Yet amid the suggestion of execution, the dead flower, and Caroline's tormented powerlessness is this single mundane habit—this *only household art*, writes Vonnegut—that she learned from her mother: pressing together pieces of soap. I don't remember what happens to Caroline, or if this soap-mottling does anything for her sad life, or what else it's supposed to represent. I only remember thinking, *this is like me.* I'm a mottled ball of soap. I'm ordinary. And like every other ordinary person, I'm the chromosomes and meta-phors of millions of humans and other organisms stretched across the globe and back through time. I'm pressing myself together, and I'm being pressed together, from bits of chemicals and traditions, niches and determinisms, with bits of the other people and their works that have always been around me. This is art, life: a fragile habit clutching threads of fate, a faltering breath amid the roar of the cosmos. Or, less astronomically, a hodgepodge of small, slippery soap-bits clinging to one another against a tide of dishwater and dirt.

Sure, it's that old alchemy, a truism, of the extraordinary in the ordinary, infinite possibilities in limited reality, William Blake's heaven in a grain of sand. But it's more. It's social, not solitary—or to use the same formula, it's the social in solitude, what makes solitude possible and gives it meaning, and the constellation of solitudes that we then idiosyncratically trace through the social to give *it* meaning. It's Ernst Bloch's utopian surplus, James Baldwin's daring love, Emily Dickinson's open door at dawn. Caroline is not so alone. Her mother taught her. And like Caroline pressing soap slivers into new bars, the only art she knows, it's not always a *choice.* Art isn't the inspired genius of a solitary individual. It's a social and political necessity, a set of evolutionary adaptations, a historical coalescence. *Everything* I read is life-changing because it all becomes a new bit of my life, a new sliver pressed into the soap, and the reading, the writing, the living holds me together.

I might also be tempted to say something about domesticity and the everyday, or something about balance and care. Vonnegut's scene is about the everyday, and it's also an everyday sort of scene—like I said, why *these* words? But why any words? Words' value isn't inside the words, but achieved through what you do with them. Same with soap, really. It's about the work, the daily habits, the livelihood. Not genius, again, but a deep want, a basic need. Maybe there's a kind of genius in all this, one we've not done enough as a culture to understand. Because without due care, soap can get waterlogged and fall apart. It can dry up and crack. It can take on so much of the dirt it's supposed to remove that it's no longer soap at all, but the opposite, something that doesn't clean but makes other things dirtier. Maybe there's some truth to all of these things. And maybe what the pressing-together of various soaps can do is to shore them all up, make them better. Like this medley of interpretations of what first seemed a paltry metaphor.

You might've seen where this was going. If every passage I've read changes my life, there must be more life-changing passages. Here are a few. In the Bible, 1 Kings 19:11–12, the Lord tells Elijah to stand on the mountain and wait for Him to pass by. Dutiful Elijah does just this: "Then a great and powerful wind tore the mountains apart and shattered the rocks before the Lord, but the Lord was not in the wind. After the wind there was an earthquake, but the Lord was not in the earthquake. After the earthquake came a fire, but the Lord was not in the fire. And after the fire came a gentle whisper." God's in the whisper. God, whatever that might mean and whatever else we might make of Him or Her, Them, is divinity, transcendence, infinity, omnipotence, creativity, power. Yet here, all this is incongruously stuffed into the nothing of a whisper. A whisper, in its ordinariness, is set against, overcomes, and is revealed to be the extraordinary. It's revealed this way in a conversation, too, in the setting-together of different things and different beings, not in a thunderous ten-commandments proclamation or from a voice crying out alone in the wilderness. So if it seems like I've strayed in moving from soap to God, like this is too fanciful, too fast and far a move to make, then we should think about what exactly we mean by *God*. Cleanliness, godliness, and all that.

Life and art are this kind of extraordinary: not a wind that tears down walls and bends trees to its might, but a whisper that comes in under all the noise, gentle yet insistent, necessary yet free. Argentine author Jorge Luis Borges wrote the short story "Funes the Memorious" about a boy, Ireneo Funes, who falls off a horse and acquires a prodigious memory. Funes remembers not just the forest, but every one of its trees, every leaf of every tree, and every time he had perceived or imagined every leaf. Funes experiences everything as free and new and life-changing, all the way down, all the time—even things that feel mundane, the same, unchanging or unchangeable. It bothers him that the word *dog* could possibly refer to so many different individuals, with different shapes, colours, and sizes, let alone all those individuals at different times, in different activities, from different angles, such as a golden retriever seen from the side as it walks in the morning and a terrier mix seen from the front as it eats in the afternoon. Introducing Funes to Caroline, we can say that even if all the moistened slivers pressed into me and my writing were somehow identical to those slivers you press into yourself, they'd be different because it would be the slivers we've so far called *me* and not the ones we've called *you* that they press up against. There's some path dependence here, some selection pressures. How, when, where, why they're pressed would make them different, too, and who finds the new ball of soap, uses it, and for what. It's social, it's mundane—it's genius and divine.

Getting back to godliness, the second-last soap-chip I'll press into this little jumble comes from the poet Anne Carson, who opens her poem "God's Justice" by observing that during creation there were days set aside for tasks. Yet on the day that God was supposed to create justice, He got involved creating a dragonfly—its turquoise dots, wire legs, eye globes, glassy polish, black wings—and lost track of time. Or did He? For, as Dickinson writes, forever is composed of nows. If we think that life should be about a wind or earthquake or fire, Justice, Art, Eternity, then we will miss the whispers, dragonflies, moments, and slivers of soap that it *is* about. The writer has a duty to preserve these ubiquitous, incongruous, extraordinarily ordinary beauties. The writer also has a duty to hold open possibility and hope, to refresh our collective imagination and reinvigorate our futures. The bleakness of Caroline's kitchen is not incidental. Whether we sit waterlogged in the soapdish, slip drop by drop through its bars, or scrub grit and grime, we witness and renew the world around us.

Garbage Trucks, the Ocean, and Single-Serve Yogurt: Or, How to Be Stabbed by Hopeless Joy

JAYA SINHA

In *A Separate Peace*, John Knowles describes conflict within the feeling born of hopeless joy. The combined effect of mornings too full of beauty and a world too full of hate make his protagonist Gene want to cry, and I understand. Hope has always been explained to me as an easy thing, like picking out what to wear. You wake up in the morning, you get out of bed, and you hope. Apparently, it's just something people do: hope that things will get better, hope that what they do matters, hope that everything means anything at all. This idea has always made me feel exceptionally stupid. Picture me, a modern Tantalus: ankle-deep in pools of hope, ripe hope-fruits hanging just above my head. It's there, I can see it, I can *see* other people eating and drinking, hope sticking to their fingers and running down their chins. I want nothing more than a fresh, bloody, slice of hope to sink my teeth into, but I just can't seem to grasp it.

This problem is especially daunting when hope is considered a prerequisite for joy. I used to think that joy had to be aimed like a gun, pointed unwaveringly at a target of hope. Joy was triggered by reason, bolstered by purpose and potential: in short, it was logical. Or in my case, *illogical*.

Several passages from *A Separate Peace* made little homes inside me, melting into my skin or sitting low in my stomach. But this passage

12

in particular rested under my tongue, turning itself over repeatedly in my mouth, demanding consideration. "Hopeless joy." The words seemed paradoxical when I first considered them; they might as well have read "airless balloons." Days after underlining the passage in my copy of the book, I still hadn't quite figured it out. That is, until I saw the garbage truck.

Garbage is one of the many things that tend to send me into an existential spiral. Sometimes, all it takes is one good look at a dumpster to remind me how completely and thoroughly fucked everything is. I mean, why on God's green Earth does anyone possibly need individually packaged, single-serving yogurt cups? So, when I saw the garbage truck blocking the path to my house one day, I immediately felt a familiar clench in my chest.

The truck had come for the dumpster: it sat just outside the residence building by my street, cans and bags and cigarette butts littered around it like sacrificial offerings. I'd never seen the dumpster actually *being* emptied, never even thought about it. But now, as I stood in front of the truck, arms crossed impatiently, it began to move. Two massive tires extended from its cab, moving with the lethargy and power of the greatest animal in the jungle of London Ontario. With a whine of metal, the fork slid forward, slotting neatly into what looked like belt loops at the dumpster's sides. The bin was lifted into the air, the truck's arms flexing back to dump its contents into the hopper.

When the Romantics wrote of *the sublime,* I hardly imagine they were talking about garbage trucks. Nevertheless, I was awestruck, clapping like an idiot by the time the dumpster touched the ground. The truck's driver, a confused-looking bearded gentleman, peeked out of his window to see his audience.

"That was cool!"

In retrospect, I could've been more articulate. But it seems that I got the point across. The man nodded, shouting back a "thank you!" as the truck pulled away. As I picked my way down the perpetually garbage-strewn path to my home, I smiled. In that moment, and in a sprinkling of moments since, I understood what Knowles meant.

Hopeless joy: as unanchored and intangible as sunlight, but just as warm. Firing the proverbial gun of joy into the air doesn't accomplish much, but it sure is a rush.

There is an underlying violence to this kind of fleeting rapture, despite — or perhaps as a necessary constituent of — the excitement. They're "stabs" of joy after all, a characterization that rings particularly true to me. Holding joy in one hand and hopelessness in the other, clutching them tight at the same time, is staggering. Intuitively, one would assume the violent energy their presence generates is borne from the Manichean battle, just like yin and yang, good or evil, or Blur and Oasis. But really, it's the peaceful coexistence between hopelessness and joy that sparks the flame. It's not "but" or "despite;" it's "and," an inexplicable "and." During the Second World War, Knowles's setting, I imagine that this "and" was intense and pervasive, ungraspably so: *the world may end at any second, and don't the stars look beautiful tonight?* But I'm presumptuous enough to think that I harboured some semblance of that magical "and" as I watched the garbage truck drive away.

It sounds benign, or even trite: "find a little joy in every day!" It's harder than that — a mountain to climb. But there's a reason Knowles calls hopeless joy "intolerable": it's letting the world make you a promise that you know it can't keep. It's going to Church even if you don't believe in God, just to listen to the choir and sit under the stained glass glinting in the sun. You don't have to abandon your cynicism; you don't even have to suppress it. You don't have to care what they're singing about. You just have to let that filtered light warm your skin and feel the music fill the room.

Though comforting, this half-done sketch of a philosophy's distant cousin still leaves the dreaded question unanswered. It's the Mick Jagger of questions, asked by all from Socrates to three-year-olds who've just been told they can't have ice cream: why? If there's no target for the bullet, why fire the gun at all? My simple answer: I don't know. My elusive, unsatisfying answer: you can't swim across the ocean.

Okay, I don't know about you, but I know that *I* can't swim across the ocean. I also know that this doesn't stop me from jumping in. When I run into rushing waves, letting ripping curls of water crash

14

into me, I'm not trying to get anywhere except further into the deep. I'm grateful for the salt as it buoys my body and burns my lungs. I don't want to be a propeller, too busy churning the water in circles to feel it cool my skin. I don't want to go anywhere. I don't want anything, except maybe to see a fish or two. I'm not saying that "the real treasure is the friends we made along the way" or "the journey is the destination." The journey isn't the destination, because there is no journey. There's no target, no vision of the future you need to reach. We don't have to save the world — we just have to live in it.

There's always a loose end, and this one takes the form of the single-serve yogurt cups that I so despise. From a distance, they represent a hedonistic nihilism near-identical to mine. Consciously or not, the act of purchasing a six-pack of Tropical Berry Explosion Surprise signifies a prioritization of one's immediate pleasure over a collective future. Who am I to talk of firing joy into the air with wild abandon and then criticize those who do exactly that? What's the difference between me and the yogurt-cuppers I so despise? Is there a difference at all?

I think, or at least I hope (which I can do in small doses), that a distinction can be made between floating in the ocean and floating in yogurt. I think that the difference is all in the grip. You can't hold too much, or too tight. You can't lock your joy between your fingers, hold it hostage in your palms. Joy can't be hoarded. Let it flutter into your palm, marvel at its beauty, don't ask it where it came from or where it's going next. Don't even think about asking when it's leaving. We can't catch it, it'll come on its own. To me, those single-serving yogurt cups are all but chasing joy around with a net: wanting mixed-berry-vanilla-coconut-adjacent slop, here and now and *easy*, no matter the cost. It's crushing joy's wings between sweaty palms in the urgency to hold onto it. That's the other thing that makes hopeless joy so *intolerable*; it's wild, directionless, completely out of our control. All we can do is watch the garbage truck, clap for the show, and let it drive away.

Finding the Centre
and Holding It

CLAIRE LE DONNE

There's a sense of hopelessness that permeates everything, if you let it. It was no longer a choice of watching the news or not watching the news. Even to go outside was to submit to the festering. Drinking-water advisories rang out as oil deals passed through caucus. Tents were pitched and then removed. Any belief in change was choked like wild grasses in buckthorn's grasp. It was all impossibly unavoidable, and yet we tried.

On one of those hopeless days in late June, I stole my sister's apple-red bike and rode across the city to meet with friends. The sun beat down unrelentingly, and bits of sweaty hair stuck to my neck under the helmet's chin straps. Everything was trampled and sad: the tires deflated, the gears jammed, and the roads cracked. I pushed along, my pedals spinning and squealing each second of the way.

The exact details of that day are fleeting and unimportant. Maybe there was a pitcher of fruit juice and the sound of strumming guitars. Perhaps there was even laughter. All I know for certain is this:

1. Everywhere I went, the despair found its way in. It seeped like muddy rain through an old pair of boots, squelching uncomfortably with each step I took. I found that even the most ugly and most beautiful things stirred little reaction within me. I stared at sidewalk vomit and public libraries and friends' faces feeling neither revulsion nor curiosity nor love. The only response was

a recursive guilt at my own apathy and then despair again.

2. I exited with a new book in my satchel, purchased on a whim while browsing discount displays. I was drawn to the cover with its slinking pink-orange-yellow typography that read *Slouching Towards Bethlehem*. I carried it home like Galahad with the Grail. It felt important, even then.

Everyone lounges on the green-grey carpet as bits of warm sunlight filter through the large windows. Despite the fact that the Montessori kids are responsible for vacuuming at the end of the school day, there are large clouds of dust when a girl does a cartwheel in the centre of the room. She has sage-green extensions woven into her braids and a shock of white stars painted on her forehead. She smiles at me, then shows me her palms, which have small indentations from pebbles stuck in the rough fibres of the carpet. A boy stands huddled in the corner, fiddling with the settings on his cameras as two teens engage in an intense game of chess before him. A group of girls with crotch-dropped jeans and battered tie-dye t-shirts watch on, entranced.

I pass by them all, searching for Marzieh in the crowd. I find her sitting at a wooden table with scissors in hand, methodically cutting out strips of paper to be handed out later in the evening, each marked with a quotation from Abdu'l-Bahá.

Marzieh is only nineteen, but she carries with her a kindness so deep that you would think her much older. If you were to walk in a room and Marzieh were there, she would greet you with a sincerity typically reserved for only the best of childhood friends, regardless of whether you'd already met. When Marzieh says, "I'm glad to see you," you ought to believe her. She is the kind of person who delights in community, who knows how to bring people together. In fact, she is the reason we have all gathered here today. She is the one who dreamed up the Coffeehouse (as we have dubbed these bi-weekly salon-esque meetings) and her guidance has allowed them to persist for three years.

I stand off in the corner and watch the hundred or so teenagers interact joyfully, clutching cups of tea and notebooks. Soon, the murmuring noise of conversation is interrupted by the ringing of a handbell, and the crowd falls silent. Marzieh stands in front of them all, a warm look in her eyes. "Hello, everyone," she says. "I'm so glad you could all make it here today! It's lovely to see so many familiar faces, plus some new ones too. Today's reading is centred around an idea I've been thinking a lot about lately called the twofold moral purpose. I'll hand out the quotes, and then we can get started with some good dialogue."

There is a thrumming feeling of collective inspiration in the air, as though anything that is discussed in this room could be made manifest out there in the world. I think to myself that Marzieh is the kind of person who understands hope.

There is a moment before the first word of any book where back-cover blurbs and half-conceived expectations mix to form an ephemeral sort of text. This text exists only in the soon-to-be reader's mind and is always bursting at the seams with potential energy. I like to think of it as a narrative Schrodinger's cat: this text can only exist so long as the actual book has not yet been read.

Having read *Slouching Towards Bethlehem*, I struggle to recall the exact shape that my Schrodinger's cat once took. Certainly, it was a hazy thing, filled with clichéd images of flower children and Jethro Tull concerts. My expectations were in line with something like eternal sunshine on a California horizon — golden, soft, and kind.

Rather than the pretty pictures I had imagined, my first impression was of Didion's articulate wit: clear, but not quite biting. It rang out with an unexpected sorrow, nearly elegiac. With those first few words, I opened the proverbial box and saw my cat lay dead. Somehow, for a moment, I had forgotten that dread was inescapable.

It was that clear voice which shocked me back into reality, the one that said she was all right with people on the outside of society, those whose fear is so intense that they make fateful and extreme commitments.

I recognized it at once as something intimately familiar, as familiar as a reflection in a mirror. Her words lodged themselves somewhere deep inside my mind. I could not rid myself of them. For weeks, I would go about my business with those sentences circling on repeat: "I know something about dread myself. I know something about dread myself. I know something about dread myself."

———————————

Marzieh tells me that difficulties are essential to living. Difficulties, she says, are not just a consequence of being alive; they exist to help us better ourselves. She asks me if I have heard the metaphor of the blacksmith.

Imagine this: you are a piece of metal, rough and unshapen. A blacksmith comes along and does as blacksmiths are wont to do. He places you within a blazing fire and then hammers you against the anvil. This experience is hot and painful, altogether not much fun. But then something happens. One day, you come out of the fire and find that you have changed. You are no longer the rough bit of metal you once were. You have been made into a finely crafted tool. And now, as this sturdy tool, you are able to accomplish tasks which you could not before. You change a flat tire. You fix a leaky roof.

That is what tests and difficulties spur. Or at least, that's what Marzieh's parents always believed. She says that their best work seemed to come when they were in devastation, not even necessarily as a mechanism of hope, but as something which allowed change to begin. So keep trudging through the fire, okay?

———————————

If Didion's account is to be believed (and I reckon that it is), then the Second Coming is already upon us. The falcon has already taken flight. The centre is not holding. With each clipped sentence, we are informed that disorder is taking hold. It is all spiralling out of control, and the gyre is only widening.

At the heart of it all is a feeling of dread. Dread that settles upon everything, all over the world; a thin whine of hysteria, underscoring each and every action. I felt it as I rode my sister's red bike, and Michael Laski felt it when he arranged his little book of poems square on the table's edge. And certainly, sick with her Dexedrine and gin-and-hot-water, Didion felt it herself as she sat down to interview Laski. And I feel it now — yes, even now — as I sit and write this too.

As it is, I cannot criticise those who, in their despair, turn to desperate and doomed commitments. It is the most natural of compulsions, as natural as the jerk of a knee when tapped with a rubber mallet. I cannot criticise any of these people and their strange compulsions: not those who collect rosaries and preach of salvation; not those who live in the numb hands of addiction; not those who quibble over ethical debates; and, certainly, not those who sit alone in their rooms writing stories. It would not be fair to judge. We all want relief.

———————

There is a certain appeal to *Slouching Towards Bethlehem* owing to its journalistic origins. I have always found journalism a beautiful intersection between art and material society. I first found this beauty as a child, sitting in the back of my father's Toyota Camry with my cheek against the cool glass window, a CBC broadcast playing cheerily on the radio. I still remember how the interviewer said, "He was contrite, yes? And then you had to cheer him up." By its nature, journalism is a collaborative effort. To tell a story, you must use many voices. It is a form of art which is community based, decidedly anti-solipsistic. Naturally, with many voices come many perspectives. A single text becomes a many-headed hydra. It gains the ability to contradict itself.

"The dread feels insurmountable. Inescapable," I say.

"There is hope, if you look for it," Marzieh replies.

When Didion walked through Haight-Ashbury, she wrote down all she saw and heard. As she transcribed each moment and conversation, they became concrete. Now, fifty-seven years later, I sit here with those conversations in my hands, nestled between the pages of a book bought on a whim. I read, considering each of those moments with care. Many are broken and sad, too full of despair to allow for anything but a sinking sensation in my chest. But then, some are not. Some carry with them a careful sort of dream, one of kindness and change. That is the beauty of writing, I think. Each written word is like a hammer, nailing the time and place and feelings of a moment down in tangibility. To write is to say: this is important, something was here. "There is hope, if you look for it." See? It is there. I have put it on paper.

And so I write. I transcribe everything I see and hear, if not for you, then for me. I write, because if I can capture the despair, then maybe I can capture the hope too. Because where do you begin in a sinking, slouching world? Where else but here?

The Quality of Mercy is Sometimes Strained

Joel Faflak

Night flight to San Francisco. Chase the moon across America. God! It's been years since I was on a plane.

When we hit 35,000 feet we'll have reached the tropopause, the great belt of calm air. As close as I'll ever get to the ozone.

I dreamed we were there. The plane leapt the tropopause, the safe air and attained the outer rim, the ozone which was ragged and torn, patches of it threadbare as old cheesecloth and that was frightening . . .

But I saw something only I could see because of my astonishing ability to see such things.

Souls were rising, from the earth far below, souls of the dead of people who'd perished from famine, from war, from the plague and they floated up like skydivers in reverse, limbs all akimbo, wheeling and spinning. And the souls of these departed joined hands, clasped ankles and formed a web, a great net of souls. And the souls were three atom oxygen molecules of the stuff of ozone and the outer rim absorbed them and was repaired.

Nothing's lost forever. In this world, there is a kind of painful progress. Longing for what we've left behind and dreaming ahead. At least I think that's so.[1]

(*Angels in America* by Tony Kushner)

---

1. Tony Kushner. *Angels in America: A Gay Fantasia on National Themes*, rev. ed. (New York: Theatre Communications Group, 2013), 285. All quotations from the play and Kushner's supplementary material are taken from this edition.

In her final monologue in *Perestroika*, Part Two of Tony Kushner's *Angels in America*,[2] Harper Pitt is finally free of lies. The Mormon wife of a closeted Mormon husband, throughout the play she imagines that the hole in the ozone is a sign of coming apocalypse both at home and across the cosmos, a double reality she both braves and disavows by taking "Lots of Valium" (32). But now she's armed with the insight that struggling to reckon with the thwarted desire of our dreams is necessary to moving forward. Speaking truth to her empowerment, she is one of the playwright's several voices for the possibility of redemption. As Kushner writes, "Words are important, and they're specific. We speak to produce effects, to catalyze, to engender consequences. We choose words strategically, precisely, whether or not we do so consciously" (315). Words matter more than ever, proving that the aesthetic always has political impact. I thus cite the monologue in its entirety because, to render it otherwise would be to sunder what is for me the nearly spiritual dimension of its saying – a transcendence that matters precisely because it comes with qualifications. Its unconditional nature only matters because it's born of conditions that make it possible.

Angels in America arrived on Broadway in 1993 in response to the US government's brutal disregard of AIDS. Dispassionate and apocalyptic, ironic and prophetic, Kushner spoke as a kind of Hebrew prophet ventriloquizing Joseph Smith, hierophant of what Harold Bloom calls the one truly American religion. Toward the end of Part One of *Angels*, *Millennium Approaches*, real-life Roy Cohn, the "polestar of human evil" (229) dying from AIDS, is visited by the ghost of Ethel Rosenberg, who announces: "History is about to crack wide open. Millennium approaches" (118). Shortly after, the Angel of America crashes through the theater ceiling to announce, "the Great Work

---

2. Part One of *Angels in America*, *Millennium Approaches*, premiered in 1991, followed by *Perestroika* in 1992. Both parts opened on Broadway the following year. They can be performed separately or together. Part One suspends its audience on the verge of a prophecy that may or may not be fulfilled. Part Two fulfills that prophecy.

begins" (125). In his "Gay Fantasia on National Themes," the play's sub-title, Kushner wields his dramatist's knife with Nietzsche's Dionysian fury tempered by Brecht's surgical precision. Given the way history goes, the "Great Work" might be either dream or nightmare. Disease, racism, homophobia, poverty, misogyny; transformation, progress, wisdom, revelation, understanding: all are imaginable outcomes, light turning to darkness, and vice versa, on a dime. Thirty years on, that uncertainty persists as the terror of not knowing if change will produce tolerance or the excoriation of all things vital to our survival.

I end every course by reciting Harper's speech to remind my students that things always seem precarious and thus to ponder the limits of forgiveness in the web of perilous times whose tensile strength is no more than "old cheesecloth" strained by crisis and catastrophe. I don't mean how late capitalist society monetizes redemption to avoid us having to think about the cost of things. That's a given. I mean contemplating *rapprochement* with our supposed enemies without eliminating the differences between us, the struggle to face the extremities of being-with as well as being-apart. As Kushner says,

> I have been blessed with remarkable comrades and collaborators: Together we organize the world for ourselves, or at least we organize our understanding of it; we reflect it, refract it, criticize it, grieve over its savagery and help each other to discern, amidst the gathering dark, paths of resistance, pockets of peace and places from whence hope may be *plausibly* expected. (333; my emphasis)

However fragile, human connection is the best we've got. Hope *must* spring eternal for us to survive, a cost we have perpetually to re-calculate.[3] Given human history, retreat also seems plausible. But to survive the onslaught, we still have "plays" as collaborative

---

3. As Kushner writes, "hope, when it can't be discovered in certainty, can always be located in indeterminacy, and *Angels* is a hopeful work" (x).

endeavors that compel our response. The ancient Dionysia reminded Greeks gathering for art was cathartic, but first it was the responsibility of all citizens.

But *how* to survive? A late scene in *Perestroika* stages Harper's final shared hallucination with Prior Walter, the play's protagonist battling AIDS, chosen to prophesy redemption from the disease. Set among the ruins of San Francisco after the 1906 earthquake, a stand-in for heaven as a place of death-like stasis where change has no purchase, Prior asks Harper to stay. Her reply:

> I feel like shit but I've never felt more alive. I've finally found the secret of all that Mormon energy. Devastation. That's what makes people migrate, build things. Devastated people do it, people who have lost love. Because I don't believe God loves His people any better than Joe loved me. The string was cut, and off they went. Ravaged, heartbroken, and free. (263)

The sheer vitality of devastation inspires Prior to return the Tome of Immobility granted by the Angel of America, his chance to check out from mortality, to avoid prophecy altogether:

> We can't just stop. We're not rocks. Progress, migration, motion is . . . modernity. It's *animate*, it's what living things do. We desire. Even if all we desire is stillness, it's still desire *for*. [. . .] Even if we go faster than we should. We can't *wait*. And wait for what? God – He isn't coming back.

Joseph Smith's God promised a Manifest Destiny that allows hopeful settlers to move westward only if they remain blind to the trauma they inflict along the way – the promise of absolute liberty as the greatest lie of all. *That* devastation.

One way to survive giving into life and change, and thus to move "past hope," is not passing judgement but straining the limits of forgiveness, perhaps the play's greatest lesson, as in the interplay between Cohn and Rosenberg, among the more reprehensible examples in American history of the struggle between adversary and victim. Two overlapping encounters in the play take this human-all-too-human litmus test further. When Harper finally leaves Joe, he pleads, "Please, please, don't leave me now" (283). Walking up to him and slapping him, she responds quietly, "Did that hurt? *(Joe nods yes.)* Yes. Remember that. Please" (283). "Please" works both ways. Joe then asks her to "Call. You have to," to which she replies: "No. Probably never again. That's how bad. Sometimes, maybe lost is best. Get lost. Joe. Go exploring." She presses two Valium pills into his hand, with instructions: "With a big glass of water." With disillusionment comes an awareness that illusions are still necessary coping strategies – as long as we don't take them for real.

The scene then shifts to Prior and Louis who, unable to deal with Prior's suffering, abandons him for Joe Pitt. Returning to ask forgiveness, he faces a different abandonment in Prior's response: "I love you Louis [. . .] I really do. But you can't come back. Not ever. I'm sorry. But you can't" (284). Perhaps unconditional love is the most toxic of human attachments, the realization we pay for being human, again without which we couldn't move forward. Like Harper's line in the sand – "*Probably* never again" – Prior, traumatized by abandonment, like God abandoning "His people," insists that things can never remain *as they were*. An opening into the future minus the illusion that things will turn out OK: death will do that to us.

I think I teach *Angels in America* because it helps me to staunch my own heart bleeding into despair. But it also reminds me, when I look into my students' faces, that despair can be stared down. That's too easily said, but it has to be imaginable. Even after the Angel of America wonders why after "the grim Unfolding of these Latter Days bring / [. . .] you or any Being should wish to endure them," a future devastation in which the "rising, scorching, unrelenting Sun" will "bare[ ] the Earth clean as bone" (277), like Harper's terror of the hole in the ozone, Prior rejects immortality:

I've lived through such terrible times, and there are people
who live through much much worse, but . . . You see them

living anyway. [. . .] But I recognize the habit. The addiction to being alive. We live past hope. If I can find hope anywhere, that's it, that's the best I can do. It's so much not enough, so inadequate but . . . Bless me anyway. I want more life (278-79).

As Harper states in her final monologue, we're merely carbon-constituted entities, carbon-dated by the imprint of a history we never asked to be born into but compelled to respond to in often irrevocably destructive ways. Gazing upon history's ruins, we're destined to endure history's "painful progress."

But to "live past hope" is also to recognize that "Nothing's lost forever." Harper's and Prior's "astonishing ability to see such things" sears our perception with an enlightenment that, as Adorno and Horkheimer remind us, "radiates disaster triumphant."[4] So, in a world in which humans toy with destruction, Prior's last words to the audience risk the impossible:

This disease will be the end of many of us, but not nearly all, and the dead will be commemorated and will struggle on with the living, and we are not going away. We won't die secret deaths anymore. The world only spins forward. We will be citizens. The time has come.

Bye now.

You are fabulous creatures, each and every one.

And I bless you: *More Life.*

The Great Work Begins (290).

The "disease" is AIDS, but it's also the disease of life itself, "the addiction to being alive," like Harper's addiction to the illusions that sustain her — until they don't. Perhaps we should ask for less

---

4. Theodor Adorno and Max Horkheimer. *Dialectic of Enlightenment* (New York: Verso, 1997), 3.

life, which, despite the poem's apparently transcendent ending, also remains a possibility, especially when the "painful progress" of life runs up against an idealism that makes impossible demands on our capacity to survive life in the first place.

As Harper's mother-in-law, the austere Hannah Pitt and most unlikely companion at Prior's side in *Perestroika*, says, "An angel is a belief. With wings and arms that can carry you. It's not to be afraid of. And if it can't hold you up, seek for something new" (242). As if not hearing what an apparently devout Mormon is actually saying to him, Prior assumes he knows what Hannah thinks of him: "I'm a homosexual. With AIDS. I can just imagine what you . . ." (240). Before he gets the chance to say "think," she checks both the thought and his thinking: "no you can't imagine. The things in my head. You don't make assumptions about me, mister, I won't make them about you." As I'm wont to say to my students, "As long as no one is burning a cross on my front lawn, I will listen to those who can't accept me for who I am, because maybe I haven't accepted them for who they are." It's not that easy, but still, still . . .

I am now 66 years old. When in 1989 I came out to my parents, the product of a generation's limited capacity for queer acceptance, they responded: "As long as you're happy, we're happy." It was a simple but powerful reassurance upon which I wasn't certain I could depend. It also turned the responsibility for happiness back in my camp. Such responses are often too pat insofar as they don't fully challenge how far we might extend forgiveness to those who are otherwise threatening enemies, especially the ones society manufactures to keep its own illusions intact, like members of the LGBTQIA+ community – who are, after all, always already members of all our communities. Whatever acceptance my parents extended – what I wish for all of my students – we still need to remember that even with acceptance there will likely be more dead bodies. Even in moments of recognition, acceptance, even revelation (which don't always correspond to one another), I remind myself and my students that the classroom signals a privilege to which others have little to no access. Still – still – we have the voice of poetry and its dramatization of life that speak from the wilderness of their saying. Amid the chaotic "akimbo" of human entanglements – violent, exhilarating, irrevocable – that are all we have to bind together the fragile "nets" of human survival, we need to hope for "More Life." At least I think that's so.

II – FREEDOM

My Obituary

BRIDGET WHELAN

Caligula was once passing a column of captives on the Latin Road when one of them, with a hoary beard reaching down his breast, begged to be put to death. "So," replied Caligula, "you are alive, then, as you are?"

(*Letters from a Stoic* by Seneca)

I first read Seneca in grade six, during recess. The October sun was warm, and I flipped through the pages on the back steps of our gymnasium. I understood little, and at the time, Caligula's question — you are alive, then, as you are? — haunted me even though I didn't fully understand the interplay between grief and self-death. All I knew: my mother was dead, and I wanted to join her.

Before I learned what death was, I sought to correct it. Convinced she was still alive somewhere, I stood on my stumpy toddler legs and bounded into the forest behind my family home. I outstretched my chubby fingers to grasp the gaps between the trees, that primordial and maternal darkness, and called, "Mommy, mommy. I'm coming to save you." Although my father carried me home, petted my hair, and sang "my little sunshine" as I drank my strawberry milk before bedtime, my eyes remained fixed on the window and the expanse beyond. I did not beg for death — death, what a harsh word; perhaps reunion or reconciliation — no, I did not beg; I ran full-throttle.

I have an instinctual urge to consume or to be consumed, a desire to sprint into a void and lose myself. When I was in middle school, I found an anglerfish dating simulation game. It was an independent art project with an eerie soundtrack and ghostly images creeping across a black monitor. A small grey male flickered on the screen. Bioluminescent strands swayed in the distance then faded. The only constant was the extensive darkness that swallowed everything like an open, gaping jaw. Engulfed in a mass of blankets and surrounded by the sounds of a city at night, I clicked the button to download the file.

A male angler fish cannot eat, and yet he is tormented by a desire to feed. The only thing that can sustain him is the flesh of a female angler, but as soon as he bites, his body melds with hers. He dissolves, becoming a bump bulging from her skin. He loses autonomy and consciousness. Is he alive, then, when he is nothing more than a grotesque protrusion? Is his insatiable urge to feast a death-wish? Is he aware of his end? I was a pre-teen when I contended with these questions, and I still have no answers.

I imagine it is a torturous life, navigating an expansive nothingness with an ever-present urge to destroy yourself. I also imagine this is what that bearded man felt when he begged Caligula for death. The urge is what I felt when I bounded into the forest intent on rescuing my already-dead mother from imagined peril. In my adolescence, I ambled through the same forest. My gait was slow, ponderous, with none of the frenzy it had a decade prior. In the wintertime, I neglected my coat to assure myself that I was alive. The sting of snow on my arms was proof: if I was cold, I must have been warm to start with, and if my body was warm, it was living. This base syllogism tempered my death-wish for a while, but it worsened with the years. I found myself dog-earing page 141 in my *Letters from a Stoic* and tracing the underlined words: "So," replied Caligula, "you are alive, then, as you are?" My answer: a resonant "no."

Even now, I question whether I am alive. At the subway station, the train rushes past me, and for a split second, my heels lift from the tile. I lean on my balcony's railing with my shoulders hanging tantalizingly over the bar as cars gush down Toronto's main artery. In my kitchen, I pause while chopping onions and admire the glint of sunset on my cleaver. I think of that man, bearded and begging, and the words "So you are alive then?" Although I disagree with Seneca's belief system, this story is a pillar of my personal philosophy. I choose to be alive. Like Stilbo — a man who lost his family, home, and freedom during an invasion, and who stared his conqueror in the eyes and said, "I have lost nothing" — I too challenge the world. I refuse to kneel in the dirt and grovel.

When I shifted my perspective, I found my mother alive everywhere — in maple keys strewn in our driveway, in the jazz music my father played late into the night, and in old family photos I secreted away and taped to my mirror. My father tells me I am just like her. He hears her voice in the lilt at the end of my sentences. When I'm angry, he sees only her anger in the muscular tension around my eyes. Even the posture I adopt when I read resembles hers. I am a body with a ghost transposed — a curled body with two identical legs pressed to my chest and two dangling off the armrest. My body houses my mother in the same way her body housed mine.

Am I alive? I don't know, but through me, she is. Through me, many people are re-animated. When my father looks at me, he sees the spitting image of my mother, but I have inherited his mannerisms. My hands fidget when I speak; I flinch from eye contact. I have even developed, against my wishes, his odd sense of humour. My eyes are an exact replica of his and his mother's before him. I stare in the mirror, and they stare back.

The body houses invisible marks as well. It collects mementos. When I walk along a dark road at night, I find myself humming my old choir tunes, and a kaleidoscope of jeweled glass refracts in my vision. Lime green flashes in the periphery, and my grade six teacher stands, once more, before me. A mob of kids surround her and vie for a pixie stick, their reward for wearing lime green, her favourite colour. My collection of recipes might as well be a newspaper obituary to everyone I've loved and lost.

My *Letters from a Stoic* is marred by pen and smudged with dirt. The book is my obituary, a time capsule, of everyone I've ever been and everywhere I've ever gone. There is a bloodstain — mine — on page 40, and on page 140, the entrails of an ant streak across the top. I have annotated the pages multiple times, and the pen strokes bear witness to time's passage. The cursive is from middle school. From high school, my letters are jagged, tall, and cramped. Now, my curves are almost spherical. They bulge from the page like protrusions or welts. I store the book with my other mementos such as my mother's name tags that my dad cut from her old uniform and the lilac stem I plucked and dried from the bush outside my childhood bedroom.

Being alive is more than a heartbeat. I live not because of my body, but because of all the people who have impacted me. I am their obituary. The question — "are you alive, then, as you are?" — still taunts me, but I believe I found my answer. The night curves around me — its darkness only broken by thin birch trees sprouting upward. Pale bark peels, flutters to the ground, and exposes dark eyes surrounding each knot on the trunk. Behind me, I hear my father's voice — "You're just like your mother. A spitting image." — then the soft lilt of jazz. The moon rises above the trees, and the forest flickers in a myriad of black and fungal white. A stream trickles nearby. A splash breaks the monotonous aqueous burbling. In one moment, I am here in the forest behind my childhood home. In the next, bioluminescent filaments sway in the distance. Up ahead, a light swings side to side. Is it a light bulb or a lure?

A Certain May Morning

Vanessa Brown

If it had not rained on a certain May morning Valancy Stirling's whole life would have been entirely different.

(*The Blue Castle* by Lucy Maud Montgomery)

When I was twelve, I read *The Blue Castle* by L. M. Montgomery so many times I lost count. When I reached the last page, I'd flip right back to the beginning. There were plenty of books to choose from at home or in the library, but that year I read *The Blue Castle,* and only *The Blue Castle.* It would become a prophetic text for my life.

L. M. Montgomery is the author of *Anne of Green Gables,* the novel that ignited my lifelong passion for books. It was 1985, and the Sullivan adaptation was on TV. That spunky redhead resonated with me, and, for Christmas, my parents gave me a box set containing *Anne of Green Gables, Anne of Avonlea,* and *Anne of the Island. Anne* was the first "chapter book" I ever read. Learning that there were eight titles in the series was my introduction to book collecting. I read every Montgomery novel I could get my hands on: *Anne,* then *Emily,* then *Pat,* then *Marigold.* L.M. Montgomery was by far my favourite writer, and in my fundamentalist Christian home, she was sanctioned. The customs and conventions of Avonlea reinforced the traditional conservative mores that formed the basis of my household and faith community. Sure, Anne talked too much. She bucked against the rules. She subverted the status quo of the sleepy little town she lived in, and she got into lots of scrapes and adventures. However, a safe, small-town boundary surrounded all these divergences from the norm. Anne still strove to be honest and good, polite and obedient. She still fell in love with a man. She still gave up her career when she married. She still valued fitting in. Most importantly, Anne learned to hold her tongue.

At its heart, the *Anne* series is one of rehabilitation towards conformity, and for good reason. The author, who maintained her Victorian values long after they went out of fashion, was much like her young heroine in that she learned throughout her life how to mask her own vibrancy and conform to society. Montgomery positioned herself as a simple pastor's wife to her friends and neighbours, despite being an internationally renowned author, independently wealthy, and the smartest person in every room she occupied. She downplayed her non-conformist qualities, fearing they might threaten her role as a traditional wife and mother. However, maintaining that image confined and limited her. The husband to whom she dedicated her life was ungrateful, jealous, and mentally ill to the point of being unable to work. Montgomery had the resources to escape her marriage. She could have moved to one of the big cities she visited and adored. She could have indulged her sexual curiosities, her fascination with the occult, and her thirst for intellectual companionship. Instead, Montgomery dedicated herself to being the wife of a man who made her life a living hell, and mother to her two sons — one of whom was an ungrateful, unemployable sexual predator — all while shelling out money to selfish relatives who took her for everything she had. She lived as a character in someone else's story. An addiction to barbiturates and alcohol was the by-product of her stressful life. She died by voluntary overdose in 1942, having sacrificed her happiness and talent all for the sake of keeping up appearances and pleasing others.

Of course, I didn't know anything about Montgomery's biography when I picked up *The Blue Castle* and read the first line, "If it had not rained on a certain May morning Valancy Stirling's whole life would have been entirely different." It is my opinion that a truly good book can be summarized effectively in a tight elevator pitch. The pitch for

The Blue Castle is as follows: A repressed woman finds out she is going to die and rebelliously decides to live life on her own terms. You've encountered this story many times in film and literature. It's not a super innovative idea, but what makes Valancy's story different is its intimacy and humour. Montgomery renders the narrative so that it is lucid and self-aware. Her heroine deftly undercuts the Victorian moral code that held the author hostage, through both grand gestures and small moments of defiance in ordinary life. *The Blue Castle* became a cautionary tale for me, infecting my adolescent brain with a life-long disease: a deep-seated and indelible fear of mediocrity, stagnation, and conformity. Like Valancy, I resolved not to follow stupid and repressive rules. Unlike Anne, I would never outgrow my urge to break free. I would strive to be different.

However, my restrictive faith system was connected to a deeply ingrained love for my family and friends. I wanted to please them. Despite all of my rebellions, as an adult I still somehow found myself living as a stay-at-home mom, keeping house for a husband I liked but did not love. I found myself attending a church whose teachings were abhorrent to me, struggling to fit into a community that just didn't get me. By this time, I was in my early thirties — older than Valancy — and desperately in need of a certain May morning to come along and change everything. Valancy reviewed her whole life between midnight and the early spring dawn. It was a very drab existence. When that night was over, something had happened to Valancy — perhaps the culmination of the process that had been going on in her mind ever since she had read Dr. Trent's letter. It was three o'clock in the morning — the wisest and most accursed hour of the clock. But sometimes it sets us free. "I've been trying to please other people all my life and failed," she said. "After this I shall please myself. I shall never pretend anything again."

In 2012, my dear friend Benjamin, an L. M. Montgomery scholar and writer, invited me to his wedding. During the reception, he and his partner Jacob presented a slideshow: happy smiling faces, arms around family members, snapshots of vacations and road trips and special dinners. I sat there, pregnant with my second child, next to my likeable husband, and realized that my life was nothing like Benjamin and Jacob's. In contrast, my life felt like a lie. When I imagined myself sitting through the same kind of slideshow at my own fiftieth wedding anniversary years in the future, other smiles in our slideshow of photos would be genuine, but mine would be fake, a well-honed construction masking my unhappiness. I didn't want my children to be raised in a deceptive pantomime. I had to do something. Hugging my friend in congratulations, I knew my life had to change if I wanted to be genuinely happy like Benjamin and Jacob.

It didn't take a letter from Dr. Trent to convince me that I had to leave my husband. All it took was the memory of a battered paperback in the hands of a twelve-year-old girl sitting in a school hallway, reading her favourite book. That little girl understood something important. It was only after I, like Montgomery, had sacrificed my own happiness and talent for the sake of pleasing others and keeping up appearances that I could really embrace what I had learned so many years before. Although my "certain May morning" did not happen in the wilds of Muskoka, or any place so romantic, there was a sea-change in my heart — a change that screamed for me to shift direction to a new port. "After this I shall please myself. I shall never pretend anything again."

Thanks to this radical redirection, I found my Barney Snaith. He's dashing, irreverent, devoted, distracting, and a little asymmetrical. We have our little house in the Mistawis — my *Blue Castle.* Crazy piles of books reside in that small house, with two dogs, two cats, three kids, and the love of my life. This amazing existence would never have materialized if I'd continued to be a character in someone else's story. Instead, I wrote my own.

Beware, for I am Fearless

CARLING DEKAY

Beware; for I am fearless, and therefore powerful.

(*Frankenstein* by Mary Shelley)

For as long as I can remember, I have been cursed with rage. Anger brews beneath my carefully crafted surface like a tea bag, steeped and bitter. Perhaps it is clichéd that my fury reached its height when I was a teenager, yet clichés are tired truths. From the ages of ten to sixteen, I felt fearlessly furious at a world more powerful than me. As a teenager, I turned to books for comfort, and I first picked up a well-worn school library copy of *Frankenstein* on a mission of self-improvement. I had spent many of my early teenage years reading Young Adult fiction and was embarrassed at how little I knew of literature published before the 2000s. Hungry for knowledge to fuel me, I attacked classic fiction as a scientist would a microscope. I delighted in learning the origins of common sayings and discovering the ways film influenced my understanding of classic texts. When I created a list of books to lead me on my journey of self-discovery, *Frankenstein* was at the top. It was a book about which I knew everything and nothing. Once I cracked its spine, *Frankenstein* became a mirror rather than a microscope.

For as long as I have been aware of how I love, I have also known society would not accept it. Schoolyard bullies and family members called me queer before I reclaimed the label. Back then, I believed the word was dirty, as was I. Being gay in a rural area is a profoundly alienating experience. With that knowledge, I became a stranger, alone and abject among family and friends. To survive, I made myself the quiet, unassuming girl. All the while, my rage simmered, seethed, and boiled, for queer anger has always felt safer than queer love.

A narrative about a man who abandons his heterosexual duties regarding marriage and children to create a being separate from society captivated me. I was both Victor, who desires knowledge beyond what society allows, and the raging solitary monster hell-bent on revenge against his forsaker. The innermost Russian doll of *Frankenstein*, the creature's tale, is wrapped in layers of storytelling, and his concealed narrative mirrored my own overboiling desires and anger. It was 2013, my household had just upgraded from dial-up internet, and queer culture was opaque to me. As I read, the story began to show me my reflection, just as the creature sees himself in a pool for the first time. The opaque became clear. It was as though Mary Shelley, who many scholars believe was also queer, wrote the book for my angry little queer soul.

The stony, shocked silence vibrated in my mom's red minivan and echoed in my head as I read the scene when Victor looks upon his creature for the first time. My revelation was like the unveiling of Victor's creature: a bell that couldn't be unrung. Yet, I revealed my truth. The mirror cracked. A stench of disgust permeated the stifling silence of the closet to which I would soon return. Today, I remain in that prison, built from my desire to make everybody as comfortable as possible. Just as Victor agrees to marry Elizabeth after he fails in his endeavour to create life outside the confines of heterosexual culture, I too played along, only ever introducing love interests as friends. I donned a chameleon mask. Forcing myself into the mould of a person I thought merited love, I forgot how to love myself.

The monster's narrative is the beating heart of Shelley's novel, and it thumps in tandem with my pulse. A creature doomed to walk the earth alone, rejected by those who ought to care for him — this story became my biography. The rage he felt over his solitary existence and unrequited longing echoed my teenage crisis. In his simple plea for a female mate to share this existence with him, he voiced a request I lacked the bravery to demand. I knew the cold the creature felt as he observed Agatha and her family. Both he and I had been exiled to the fringes of firelight, banned from basking in its warm glow. Like the creature, I tried to discover myself through books (though I was not, like the creature, reading Milton, Plutarch, or Goethe). I gazed at my image and saw a monster staring back. The mirror revealed a girl that was both me and nothing like me. She hid behind curtains of long hair and wore clothing that made her as invisible as possible. Once, my eighth-grade teacher pulled my mother aside and expressed concern about my lack of pride in my appearance. Puberty only exacerbated this dissatisfaction. Even today, I cover most of the mirrors in my house, because the image looking back is never quite right.

I longed for a companion as the creature does: someone to love and to love me in return. Rage replaced longing when the world denied my request. I took the creature's tirade against Victor — "Beware; for I am fearless, and therefore powerful" — as a personal motto. With anger as my guide, I set up a queer alliance at my school. As the only semi-out attendee, I tried new gender expressions by wearing many hats. Untethered from the lies that composed the walls of my yellow brick childhood home, I let myself be queer. Queer friends, well-versed in doublethink, permitted me for the first time to be loud and angry. They showed me a monster could be lovable and loved.

Frankenstein is not a triumphant queer allegory. The creature makes good on his promise to kill Elizabeth before she and Victor can consummate their marriage. For fear of increasing the monster's stock, Victor refuses to grant his creature a female counterpart. Locked in mutual hatred, creature and creator careen toward tragic deaths. For a child who did not believe in happy endings, this disastrous dénouement was everything. *Frankenstein* showed me who I was and who I could become. Because of that story, I was able to break free from my glass prison and build a home with the jagged pieces. Mary Shelley's story launched my queer journey and gave me an audacious craving for my own happy ending.

Victor doesn't give his monster a name, but I named mine. I now feel more queer love than queer hate. I craft language that expresses who I am and who I want to be. Though my rage burns on, it fuels my yearning for a world where love is stronger than hatred. For the first time since my teen years, I derive a sense of euphoria from the way I present myself. My clothing choices are no longer restricted by the concern that people might think me queer. From flower crowns to graphic t-shirts celebrating queer stories, I find my way out of my closet through the garments inside it.

I'm writing my own love story: one without most family but with plenty of loud friends. Rather than drowning in the chorus of those who have abandoned me, I learned to find quiet peace in the occasional solitude of queerness. The mirror still reflects the monster I try to love. Even as I type, I sense lingering expectations of heterosexuality in each keystroke. Nevertheless, urges to be that lost little girl who hid her rage in smiles which never quite reached her eyes yield to the truth Mary Shelley taught me long ago. Beware world, the monster you made is fearless and therefore powerful.

The Art of Not Cleaning

E.J. NASH

The Mole waggled his toes from sheer happiness, spread his chest with a sigh of contentment, and leaned back blissfully into the soft cushions. "What a day I'm having!" he said. "Let us start at once!"

(*The Wind in the Willows* by Kenneth Grahame)

In the spring of 2020, I found myself in a small studio apartment with a perpetual ant infestation and an upstairs neighbor obsessed with a variety of nocturnal activities — perhaps basketball or Irish dancing, judging from the noises that came from above. This was a time of social distancing and quarantining, when I disinfected my doorknobs and used plastic gloves when grocery shopping. I was scared.

During times of stress, I turn to fiction. Perhaps this is no surprise to any fan of stories; it is far easier to jump into someone else's problems than to deal with one's own. How convenient to know that the troubles will only last for 300 or so pages. Everything will end. There will be a conclusion.

I gained a foothold on normalcy once the Ottawa Public Library reopened for curbside pickup. Then came the hardest part: finding a book to read during a crisis. This was not a time for zombies or anything apocalyptic.

In the end, I selected *The Wind in the Willows* by Kenneth Grahame. A few weeks earlier I had seen it on a list of the greatest English books of all time. I figured that a children's book would be a light way of passing the time in my claustrophobic apartment. (Once, when I sneezed, my next-door neighbor sent me a text that said, "Bless you.") I was desperate for a world with no nosy neighbors, no broken elevator.

The opening pages introduce the Mole, who is awfully busy. He brushes and dusts and sweeps in a fit of spring cleaning. And then, in a fateful moment, "something" beckons him outside. He throws down his brush, scrabbles through his tunnel, and emerges into a sunlit meadow. Moments later, the Mole meets the Rat, and they spend the afternoon boating down the river and having a picnic.

Momentarily overcome with emotion, I had to put down the book. How joyous! To throw away the cleaning, the chores, and the never-ending to-do list would be nothing short of a self-made miracle. Saying no to the pressure of perfection can be a radical act.

In those early pages, I recognized myself as the Mole. I was so caught up in cleaning and sanitizing and keeping things ordered that I had lost sight of what it meant to truly engage with the world. More than anything, I wanted to be on that boat.

Looking out my tenth-floor window, I realized that I could have something very similar to the Mole's experiences. The Ottawa River began at Lac des Outaouais and ended at the St. Lawrence; in the middle of that journey, it flowed by my apartment building. From my window, I could see gleaming shards of water in the summer and the tendrils of fog that hovered over its banks in winter. Over the years, I had cultivated the personality of one who shunned the outdoors — I joked that my version of interacting with nature would be drinking sangria on a patio.

For the first time in months, I stopped cleaning. I put down my weapons against fear — my broom, my Lysol, my hand sanitizer.

I stepped outside.

The river was a source of continual movement, not only in the Remic Rapids that stretched across the provincial border, but also in the life that thrived on its shores: the murmur of the leaves of a silver maple, the call of the red-winged blackbird, the splash of a mallard climbing up rocks. I experienced the encyclopedia of nature as I walked along the path. Only when I splashed through the puddles that crept onto the rocky shore did I realize that I had robbed myself of something primordial.

Countless bikers and joggers passed by on these walks. I wanted to grab one of them and shake them by their shoulders. "Where have I been?" I wanted to ask. "Why did no one tell me?"

During my second reading of *The Wind in the Willows*, I saw that the river becomes a guiding force taking characters wherever they need to be. In one notable chapter, the Otter's son is missing. The Mole and the Rat decide to look for him and begin their journey down the river.

They begin to hear the most beautiful of sounds. "The merry bubble and joy, the thin, clear, happy call of the distant piping!" cries the Rat. "Such music I never dreamed of, and the call in it is stronger than music is sweet! Row on, Mole, row! For the music and the call must be for us." They come to a small, dreamlike island. Here, they encounter the piper, the most incredible of beings. His curved horns, his bearded face, and his majestic essence astound and dumbfound the Mole and the Rat. Although never explicitly named, our friends have undoubtedly come across the god Pan, who traditionally reigns over nature and the wild. He is a benevolent deity who stands over the lost otter. Moments later the Mole and the Rat are blinded by a flash of the sun, and the god disappears. They are left with a vague sense that something wonderful has happened — "something very surprising and splendid and beautiful."

From this sublime experience I gained the ability to step back and enjoy the river's natural beauty. Of course, I certainly wouldn't boat down the Ottawa River. Given my terrible sense of direction, I would collide with the hydroelectric dam only a few kilometers away. But who needs a boat when one has the gifts of the wild?

The Mole and the Rat's adventure certainly could never have been experienced by someone who spends every minute cleaning and working. It was the Mole's initial decision to try something new that ultimately led him to such a profound moment.

There seems to be inordinate pressure to finish the various tasks we assign ourselves. Answer the emails, listen to the voicemails, put in the laundry, wash the dishes, vacuum the carpet, take out the garbage, fold the sheets, answer the dentist who has been trying to book an appointment for six months; by the time one chore is checked off, another has taken its place. Somehow, a list becomes a cycle. But who are we if that's all we do? Who are we if we never meet Pan the piper, who plays the essential music?

Trying something new, exploring somewhere different; these are easy to say and difficult to do. I was the type of person who always ordered the same thing at the same restaurant. By my third year in Ottawa, I could walk into the Swiss Chalet on Merivale Road, and the waiter would know what to bring: quarter chicken dinner, white meat, fries, hold the bun — thanks!

Wandering down the river was an enlightening and exhilarating moment for me. I did something that was not on my list: a foreign concept. There were no guidelines that told me to investigate the rock sculptures that hug the pathway; there were no instructions that told me to sit in the red Adirondack chairs that overlook the water. Thoughts of washing floors and scrubbing counters were far behind.

My joy in those moments reminded me of the Mole's complete submersion in his own delight. He is not stuck in the past, thinking of the work he has abandoned. Instead, he is entranced by the moment and eager for the day ahead. This idea was revolutionary. I lived in a frenzy of fears that rarely came to pass. And despite various misadventures — both the Mole and the Rat fall into the river, and their lunch is a little wet — they become closer friends in the end. The Mole has not only said yes to the outdoors; he has said yes to personal exploration, to mistakes, to dealing with consequences with kindness.

Of course, the Mole does not completely abandon his previous life. A later chapter finds him enjoying the comforts of his old underground home. He recognizes that he will return above, as he does not want to "turn his back on sun and air," but he is glad to find that there was something familiar to welcome him back.

The Mole's final lesson is profound: the ability to balance the relief of being home and the jubilation of exploring the natural world. There are times when, yes, I must clean the fridge and scrub the oven. But nowadays I will occasionally tuck away my cleaning supplies and head outside, where I seek a piper who plays the most heavenly music.

To "have lopt & cropt so successfully": Austen's Model of Creative Pursuits

Sarah Pesce

"All this she must possess," added Darcy; *"and to all she must yet add something more substantial in the improvement of her mind by extensive reading."*

(*Pride and Prejudice* by Jane Austen)

Every January 28th, I note the anniversary of *Pride and Prejudice* and give thanks for the book that changed the trajectory of my life. Reading was my thing as a kid, so much so that I cultivated an identity as a Reader — the fastest, the most voracious, the most likely to have her nose stuck in a book during recess. And sure, many a girl who grew up a Reader probably loved *Pride and Prejudice* and wanted to be as charming and witty and quick with a comeback as Elizabeth Bennet. (Sadly, every internet quiz that determines "Which Bennet Sister Are You?" never says I'm Elizabeth.) But my love of reading, and of *Pride and Prejudice* specifically, also put me on the path to personal and professional fulfillment and gave me the ability to live a creative life that Austen wanted for herself.

As an awkward teenager, I was a Reader who thought classic literature was the height of sophistication, and the Austenmania of the mid-nineties hit at exactly the right time. With an abundance of filmed adaptations that came out of Hollywood and the UK — the land-mark BBC *Pride and Prejudice* miniseries (1995), Ang Lee's *Sense and Sensibility* (1995), BBC's *Persuasion* (1995), and three different *Emma* adaptations: ITV's version with Kate Beckinsale (1996), the film with Gwyneth Paltrow (1996), and the modern American retelling *Clueless* (1995) — my Reader person was in her pretentious, classic lit element. Of all the books I read during that time, *Pride and Prejudice* was the one that adhered to me. Between Elizabeth's sass, Darcy's transformation, and the love story, I was hooked.

I read that cheap $3.99 paperback that I picked up at the bargain table at a suburban Coles at least twice a year after that first introduc-tion to *P&P*, or just whenever I needed a comfort read. I now have a collection of *P&P* editions, from informative scholarly versions for the footnotes to pretty hardbacks for bookshelf aesthetics, but that ratty paperback, with its translucent pages worn soft with use, is still my favourite. The story has been with me at every stage of my life — from first love to the confusion and loneliness of early adulthood to marriage and motherhood and beyond — and every time I read, I find new insights that deepen my experience of the book in that particular moment of my life. (After having a child, for example, I found new sympathy for Mrs. Bennet for wanting her children safe and protected and new fury at Mr. Bennet for his indolence.)

Because Austen never really left the cultural zeitgeist, her work is always being re-imagined. A web series adaptation, *The Lizzie Bennet Diaries*, was airing serially on YouTube while I was pregnant with my child, and it became an obsession that led me to fan fiction. When I ran out of fan fiction there (you can, in fact, run out of fanfic if your obses-sion is real and voracious), I went to fan fiction of *Pride and Prejudice* in general, and quickly learned that I would never run out again. There was a years-long backlist of online stories about Darcy and Elizabeth and company, and since Jane Austen wasn't going to be writing more about them, I'd happily read other people's stories, especially while on maternity leave, when I needed to do something to exercise my brain other than making a stuffed animal dance to Beyoncé.

At first I was reading. Then I was commenting on ongoing stories that were posted chapter by chapter. Then I was chatting with the authors directly. Then I was beta-ing (being a test reader for the author, and in my case, because of my background in English and my perfectionist tendencies, a *de facto* editor) for authors before they posted. Writing my own fan fiction was not in the cards for me; it was enough to enjoy and then be involved in the creation of these stories.

Then, I was back to working from home at a deeply unfulfilling job and spent a lot of time staring at the wall and wanting to do something more interesting, more rewarding, more enjoyable. In the meantime, though, I had entertainment, community, and a creative outlet online. When the people I was a beta reader for suggested I look into editing as a profession, I started researching. There was a thriving cottage industry in published Jane Austen fan fiction (JAFF) after the online self-publishing boom of the early 2010s, but maybe not enough to dedicate an entire business to JAFF. But I was reading romance at the same time I was reading fanfic, and there's a strong link between the two. JAFF is overwhelmingly about the relationship between Darcy and Elizabeth, though virtually every other imaginable pairing is also represented. And there is of course a strong link between Austen and romance. The bloodline of the modern romance industry starts with Austen as a mother figure, and runs through Georgette Heyer and her trailblazing Regency romances in the '30s and '40s, to the historical so-called bodice-rippers of the '70s and '80s that solidified the genre as a dominant force in the publishing industry.

So I would specialize in romance and in JAFF. A business licence, a website, and a leap of faith later, Lopt and Cropt Editing was born. A friend named it by suggesting a phrase from Austen's letters on editing *Pride and Prejudice*: "I have lop't and crop't so successfully...that I imagine it must be rather shorter than '*Sense and Sensibility*' altogether." If *Pride and Prejudice* was Austen's "own darling child," a source of creativity, hope, and money, Lopt and Cropt was mine. And I would have a career where I could spend my days reading. (Would Darcy think me accomplished? Maybe, though I would almost certainly shock his Regency-era sensibilities with most of the stuff I edit, some of which have him in very compromising positions.)

As a woman living in the twenty-first century Western world, I had far fewer barriers in developing this creative career than Austen did. Austen luckily had a benevolent family to help support her career, but she was hamstrung by social mores and circumstances, living in a time when most women could not legally own property or seek out work that could demonstrably change their situation without their respectability being called into question. Similarly, her characters wrestle with the fear of being beholden to men's wealth to protect them. Elizabeth doesn't need a rich husband, as she tells Charlotte Lucas in Chapter 6, but she wants to marry prudently and therefore eventually dismisses Wickham and Colonel Fitzwilliam as partners. Elinor Dashwood in *Sense and Sensibility* is even more careful, willing to let a love match with Edward Ferrars sink because they can't afford to live together on his income combined with her own meagre fortune, and only a job offer from Colonel Brandon secures their marriage. Money, and how much one has and the power that it affords them, is a concern that runs through all of Austen's novels and through her own life.

Despite her family's attempts to glorify her as someone who wrote for pleasure and to appease her natural genius rather than for financial reward, Austen herself wanted to earn money from her writing and have it read widely. Reliant on the kindness of her brothers to keep their unmarried sister from genteel poverty, Austen used her talent to attempt to create some kind of financial independence. From her tiny writing table in the busy sitting room at Chawton Cottage, through constant interruptions from visitors and servants, Austen could gaze out the window and dream about the fame and fortune that she'd never see in her lifetime. While modern readers revere Austen as one of the pre-eminent English-speaking female novelists who set the example of a successful writer, in truth, she did not earn as much as one would expect. Austen sold *Pride and Prejudice* for £110, and felt that wasn't enough, telling a friend she "would rather have had £150" for it. All in all, Austen made somewhere between £600 and £700 from her work in her lifetime, not enough to be fully independent or a wealthy woman. And while *P&P* enjoyed some popularity while she was alive, it was much later that Austen (who published as "a Lady") posthumously established her place in the Western canon and achieved long-standing commercial success.

The business of Austen these days, however, is an ironic reversal of the very modest professional wins she had in her lifetime. Today Austen is practically a guaranteed money-maker — slap her name or her characters' names on something, and it'll sell, whether it's a T-shirt with the iconic peacock cover, Post-it notes, journals, lip balms, candles, mugs, wine glasses, vases, tote bags, pretty editions of the original books, or adaptations in print or film (all of which are currently in my possession). The woman is on the UK £10 bill — the same amount for which she originally sold (and later bought back, with her brother's help) the copyright of what became *Northanger Abbey*, not released until after her death.

Even though Austen's lifetime earnings were not nearly as much as she deserved, her desire to live a creative life makes her an inspiration in terms of genius and legacy for me and for countless others. The writers I work with — almost exclusively women — have made or are striving to make a living off their creativity, or to supplement their income from their non-writing jobs. I have built a full-time career as a romance editor, reading and analyzing manuscripts and finding creative solutions to help writers produce the best book possible. Supporting ourselves through creative pursuits and forging new avenues to financial and artistic freedom, we are able to live Austen's dream. Austen's legacy isn't only the six books she wrote, or the way her writing remains popular and relevant two hundred years later; it's also her striving to make her talents work for her that continues to motivate others and make their passion their ticket to creative and financial freedom.

III – ENCHANTMENT

A Spark From Heaven

HOPE GRIFFORE

Come, shepherd, and again begin the quest!

(*The Scholar Gypsy* by Matthew Arnold)

Half of North America experienced a total solar eclipse the day Brescia University College held its final classes. Interesting coincidence, don't you think? I remember how excited everyone was. The news recycled static safety warnings. Elementary schools closed early to reduce the risk of retinal damage in children. Local libraries ran out of plastic sunglasses. My friend took the day off work to drive west with her boyfriend, chasing a clearer view of the sky.

I stayed behind. Brescia was all I could think about. Plus, I'd promised to watch the eclipse with Oscar Wilde.

Well... sort of.

Oscar Wilde was actually my professor, Monika Lee, who arrived in full costume that day to commemorate Brescia's final classes. At first, I couldn't believe what I was seeing: my professor, famously brilliant, dressed in a plum-coloured hat, purple neck scarf, and black leather gloves. She carried a short walking stick and wore a long, swirling cape. As I write this piece, zooming in on a photo from that day, I even notice a green carnation pinned to her vest. Of course. What fantastic attention to detail. The entire class adored the charade—how could we not?

While Oscar Wilde delivered a well-researched lecture that day, I honestly can't remember the specifics of it now. Monika had a strict no-electronics policy in her classroom, which meant I inevitably lost all my pencil-written notes to abandoned, half-filled binders crammed in cardboard moving boxes. Luckily there were only fifteen of us in that class (a term seminar on the Brontës), so I could always reach out to one of the other students for a copy of their handwritten notes. Most of us had known each other since our very first class together with Monika four years prior. We were nineteen then: passionate and full of run-on sentences (Monika was quick to fix the latter).

Brescia, if you didn't know, was Canada's last women's university. It closed with almost no warning on May 1st, 2024. Even the faculty was blindsided. No amount of protesting could save our campus because the decision had already been made behind closed doors.

It's strange, what your mind chooses to remember. I know, for example, that the far right window was cracked open a few inches during my last class with Oscar Wilde. Birds chirped on blooming magnolia trees beyond the glass, unaware our school was being closed while we were still inside. Oscar Wilde adjourned class at 11:30 am, meaning we had a few hours before the eclipse. Autopilot-wandering brought me to Clare Hall, the student residence that overlooks the Medway Valley Heritage Forest. Behind the building is a small fire pit surrounded by mushroom-speckled logs and tall, yellow grass.

I was only mildly surprised to find a few of my classmates already there – some sprawled out on the wet grass, lying atop coats, others conversing near the fire pit. It took less than an hour for the entire class to trickle out, one by one. I guess we all had the same idea. Even Oscar Wilde was soon chatting among us, reminiscing of her early teaching years. We traded memories, occasionally glancing upwards to see if the sky was starting to darken.

Ah! do not we, wanderer! await it too?

Being so near the forest, I was reminded of a different course on nineteenth-century British literature that I took with Monika two years prior. Midway through the second term, when energy was low, she decided we should go searching for the 'Scholar Gypsy.' According to myth, the Scholar Gypsy was an Oxford student who dropped out of university in the mid-17th century to live in the woods. Memorialized in a famous poem by Matthew Arnold, some say he continues to roam the woods, disillusioned and half-forgotten, still tired of knocking at preferment's door. So one afternoon in early March, while a misty rainstorm was blanketing London, Ontario, we prepared to start our search. Having discussed our plans the week before, we all arrived to class in rubber boots and plastic coats. Monika scribbled "heading to the woods to look for the scholar Roma person" on the blackboard, as though that were a perfectly reasonable explanation for confused latecomers.

We trekked right past the fire pit that day and into the woods, Monika leading the way. She was wearing a bright yellow raincoat, a long striped scarf and heavy-duty brown hiking boots. Her golden-furred dog trailed merrily beside us on a green leash. The paths were muddy and the visibility was awful, so we moved slowly, scanning the foliage for a glimpse of the Scholar Gypsy.

Go. For they call you.

Eventually we reached the top of a steep cliff that overlooked a narrow and shallow stream veining away from the Thames River. We all decided this would be a good place to read the poem, so we gathered around Monika, finding low-hanging tree branches, decaying stumps and mossy rocks to rest on.

Thou hadst one aim, one business, one desire...thou possessest an immortal lot, and we imagine thee exempt from age.

We listened silently. Monika's words filled the forest, weaving through the tree branches while rain dripped softly from the leaves, as if nature itself had paused to hear her.

Still nursing the unconquerable hope...

But that was a long time ago. I want to say this memory was immeasurably special, but that was more or less a regular day with Monika. She never did anything halfway. When I took a creative writing class with her, she insisted we do something to inspire the soul, so we hosted a literary-themed dinner party. She arrived dressed as Natasha Rostova from Leo Tolstoy's *War and Peace*. I was Ophelia, my favourite Shakespeare character, while others arrived as Sherlock Holmes and Victor Frankenstein. We spent the evening gathered around our potluck meal, sharing stories and trading book recommendations.

A different year she drew a valley of flowers on the blackboard (lopsided lilies, spiraled vines, something vaguely resembling a daffodil) to perform a dramatic reading of Alfred Tennyson's "Tithonus." Several professors have told me poetry is meant to be read aloud, that its sound is half its beauty. Yet none of them, aside from Monika, have ever read a poem to us with such passion that they fell to the floor in divine agony.

When I took Monsters, Ghosts and Demons of the nineteenth century with her, the class went and saw a local production of "Finding Hyde" – an imagined sequel to Robert Louis Stevenson's *The Strange Case of Dr Jekyll and Mr. Hyde*. The Palace Theatre wasn't close to Brescia, but late October we all managed to find ourselves there, seated several rows from the stage, clutching a yellow playbill in quiet anticipation. The show was eerie and electric, full of moral tension. We left buzzing with conversation. Monika stood with us just outside the entrance afterwards, coat pulled tight, delighting in our theories about duality and madness. We never imagined then that Brescia was in danger of closing.

Eventually the sky began to darken, and Oscar Wilde suggested we move to higher ground. The change in light was slow but unmistakable – a grey blanket over a warm lamp. The people around me fell silent. We took turns with the glasses, each person looking up for a few seconds before passing them on. Time seemed to slow, even the birds were quiet.

So the eclipse came and went. Our school followed suit. I was surprised by how quickly people moved on. Trash cans filled with plastic sunglasses, and my friend who ditched work said she was generally underwhelmed by the whole event. I guess I was too. Brescia had stood through more than a century of skies. It was odd to think this would be the last one.

But what—I dream! Two hundred years are flown since first thy story ran through Oxford halls.

I like to think the Scholar Gypsy was watching us that day, lingering just out of sight. Perhaps he understood, before we did, that Brescia's magic was never in its walls, but in every mind it set searching. It was never about what we found—it was always about how we searched, and who we became in the looking.

So come, shepherd, and again begin the quest!

Embracing the Hobbit Within:
One Transformative Summer
with Bilbo Baggins

MONIQUE BETTENCOURT

The dragon is slain. The battle is won. The King Under the Mountain rests eternally, the Arkenstone laid atop his chest. A gentle hobbit — undoubtedly far from his hobbit-hole — gazes one final time upon the Lonely Mountain. He has completed his adventure; his warm hearth and armchair call out to him now. With a parting remark, he turns toward home.

I first read Tolkien's *The Hobbit* when I was fifteen years old, on a flight to an island in the middle of the Atlantic. Surrounded by fellow travellers, I felt utterly alone. Five hours later, I would land and see my extended family waiting at the gates. I was petrified but simultaneously excited to have an adventurous summer.

Oh, what a summer! I lived two adventures during that trip: one unfolded with my family on a lush island, and another transported me to the fantastical Middle Earth of Tolkien's creation. Every day I busied myself outside the house — lazing on the beach, hiking overgrown tropical trails, and wandering cobblestone streets. I found my first love — or what I thought was love at the time. But every night, I came home to *The Hobbit*. Only upon closing the book could I begin to grasp the impact of Tolkien's words. Bilbo comes away from his adventure a different hobbit, and I came away from *The Hobbit* a different girl.

The Hobbit changed my life in several ways. Never again will I come across a circle without thinking of the door to Bag-End. Show me a round window, an embroidery hoop, or even a fishbowl, and my mind will conjure green panels, a round brass knob, and a secret mark carved into fresh paint. Tolkien rewrote the pages of my life, leaving me bold and unafraid to tell the stories in my mind. *The Hobbit* laid the foundation for a better version of myself.

The Hobbit taught a life-altering lesson: that every story is an adventure, and every adventure is a story. I have always been a storyteller — a theatrical orator, more precisely, but a storyteller nonetheless, who sees stories everywhere, every day. The most ordinary of encounters can ignite a spark in my brain, and a spark is all it takes for a plot to flourish. Weaving tales that captivate an audience is a source of personal pride, but for a long time I had an audience of only one. My early fictions never made it beyond the border of my mind, not because they were too precious to share, but because I deemed them unworthy of being written down — the characters too simple, the scope too narrow. But when I read *The Hobbit*, I realized I was depriving myself of the opportunity to bring entire worlds to life. Although I could not hope to be Tolkien, he inspired me to write my stories — to put them on paper and give them a beginning, middle, and end. No longer would I let my creations exist solely as free-floating tidbits of lore and prose. Besides, I had never *completed* a story before I read *The Hobbit*, so perhaps it also taught me the importance of endings, of the journey, and a journey has a destination. Pre-*Hobbit*, my endings were rife with vague generalizations and clichés — merely shadows of true conclusions. Post-*Hobbit*, I try to write emotionally rich endings with airs of finality. I want my readers to step away from my work with souls stirred and hearts cracked open, as I did when I finished *The Hobbit*.

I remember a passage from the penultimate chapter of *The Hobbit* — one of my favourite parts of the book. Atop the mountain, there is snow, untouched by the blood and fire of the battlefield below. I like to think of that snow as a soothing balm after the atrocities of war and dragon fire — a white shock blanket tucked securely around the shoulders of the Company. When feeling poetic, I see the snow as a reminder that purity can prevail, even amidst horror and tragedy.

While our world may not boast the dragons of Tolkien's Middle Earth, it is not without beasts. Dragons, demons, trauma — are they not synonymous in the end? I'm no stranger to pain, illness, death, and sadness. But Bilbo tells us that even such troubles, figuratively represented as dragons, end. My personal battle with darkness came to its eventual resolution and left me with a mind clear enough to see that every tragedy must come to a close, if I hold on until the curtain falls. A fine member of the Company I would have made, with a mindset like that.

The Hobbit made me braver, too. I went into the book a Baggins — a quiet homebody with little inclination to venture beyond my four walls and emerged from the book a little more daring and a lot less afraid of the voice in my head urging me to see the world. Perhaps, it was more than coincidence that led me to pick up The Hobbit on holiday. I know that when I closed the novel for the final time, I was more a Took than a Baggins: although you could not pay me to do anything intensely physical or spend all that time outdoors, I was willing to experiment, to explore, and to stray beyond my comfort zone. Maybe it was my inner Took that dove into a whirlwind romance with a boy from the island. My Tookishness is probably also to blame for my tendency to hop in my car at three in the morning and head out of town or for impulsive four-hour trips to my dad's Georgian Bay cottage. This Tookish side probably shoved me out of the closet and urged me to kiss a girl in a bowling alley. If not for that push of bravery from The Hobbit, I might have forever lived as a timid, quiet girl oblivious to the thrills of the world outside her bubble. My former Baggins-esque personality and my transformed Tookish self are worlds apart. I must say, living with a touch of Tookishness is fun.

Nearly a decade ago, I turned the first pages of The Hobbit during a long, lonely plane ride, read the opening lines, and found myself on a transformative journey. My adventures in Middle Earth fundamentally changed my character. The sun set on my time as a Baggins and then came the dawn of my Tookish life.

More Real Than This Schoolroom

MONA MARTIN

"When I am telling it," she would say, "it doesn't seem as if it was only made up. It seems more real than you are — more real than this schoolroom. I feel as if I were all the people in the story — one after the other. It is queer."

(*A Little Princess* by Frances Hodgson Burnett)

What is identity and where are its boundaries? Are we what we think we are, what others think we are, or something else entirely? Tennyson wrote, "I am part of all that I have met," and he's probably right. I suspect that becoming other people, whether real or fictional, is how we transform personalities into lived experience.

I began reading *A Little Princess* in June of Grade Five, and at the end of the month, I had to return the small Puffin paperback to the library without finishing it. The aborted novel, with its yellowed pages and rough drawings, took possession of me, because like Sara Crewe, I was an odd child who lived in her imagination and baffled other people's comprehension. Like Sara, I was small, skinny, and large-eyed, born into relative privilege and ease. Like her, I told stories from my earliest remembrance and had an ability to captivate an audience. A small following of friends and acquaintances, in school corridors and summer camps, asked me for more stories.

The library copy dropped into the book return bin with a heavy thud. The story had just reached the point when the once rich and petted Sara was penniless, hungry, and cold. Her acquaintances shunned her; she lived alone in the school's attic, where, to give herself courage, she pretended to be a prisoner of the Bastille and befriended a rat she named Melchisedec. My heart hurt for this fictional child — orphaned, impoverished, destitute, and alone — yet I was in awe of her heroism: how she contrived to live ethically and to give her meagre food supply to a beggar who was hungrier than her, how she nurtured the other abject and bullied students in the school, how she cared for Becky the scullery maid, and how she disdained to sink to the vindictive level of her enemies or to reveal her anguish. She maintained her dignity, even when she was derided, mocked, treated cruelly, and denied comfort. I think that I must have been born proud, and pride can easily lead to selfishness. Therefore, her pride and self-regard, which produced virtuous actions rather than conceit, struck me as beautiful, if not downright miraculous in the face of so much hostility and deprivation.

Sara's predicament hit close to home, partly because there was a group of older girls who followed me around the schoolyard at recess and mocked me. They called me "Richie," presumably because I wore the clothes my parents bought, mostly skirts and dresses, not the jeans with holes which were so popular, apparel which, despite my love of dresses, I coveted. The bullies tugged on my skirt and pulled on my coat while they asked me if my clothes came from a thrift store. Although they never hit me, their words were sharper and more wounding than the stones thrown by another notorious schoolyard bully who eventually landed himself in prison for raping a blind-deaf woman in an elevator.

Finches, robins, and pigeons populated the leafy trees, and the corn in the fields was already a foot high. After returning Hodgson Burnett's novel to the library that June, I trudged, disconsolate, along the dirt road from my school to our house. In vain, I told myself that in two short months, I would sign the paperback out and finish reading it, and that the holidays would fly by. However, the summer did not pass rapidly; the long hot unscheduled days with farm chores, housework, and swimming lessons were languorous, even tedious, and, although I did read other books, *A Little Princess* had seeped into my consciousness in mysterious ways. I began to imagine I was Sarah Crewe, whose "trick of pretending things was the joy of her life."

My drafty bedroom became the attic in Miss Minchin's school, my hard twin bed was Sara's narrow cot, and I heard our house's actual mice scurrying and scratching in the walls, just as Sara did in the school attic. Our parents gave me many chores, and I picked long rows of beans in the hot sun, mowed the lawn, washed dishes, fed the animals, and pulled weeds with better grace than usual because of Sara Crewe's uncomplaining service. I thought about being Sara so consistently and intensely that my child-mind wondered if we were one person. As she says, "If you suppose anything hard enough it seems as if it were real."

At night I imagined a variety of plotlines for the second half of the book, but the magic came from living through each of these during my waking life. Papa was really alive, and I was a stowaway on a ship to go find him. I was an actual prisoner in the Bastille and Melchisedec the rat was a prince under enchantment. Becky the scullery maid turned out to be my long-lost sister and an heiress. I became a revered French teacher in Miss Minchin's school. *Et cetera.* For those of you who haven't read the book, none of those things happens in it. Still, I've been working on living out those narratives ever since. Proud of being strange, Sara/Mona is one who mines her imagination for salvation and comfort, who strives to help others, whose self-respect acts as a kind of armour against derision, and whose ethical actions and impulses matter, whether anyone knows about them or not. Furthermore, the children's novel gave me permission to inhabit my reading fully, authentically, and profoundly. After the novel colonized my imagination, it launched an empire which changed my life. No longer the school library's story, it became mine.

Much can be traced back to this one fictional character who captivated me and shaped the waking dream of life. I became a French teacher and continued to write and tell stories, sometimes publishing them. A commitment to the world of imaginative language led to three university degrees in French and English literature. I volunteered in the community — in a hospice for pregnant teens and in an orphanage for trafficked Indigenous children. Friends come to me when they're sad, lost, or in trouble: the Lotties, the Beckys, the Ermengardes. My predilection for the heirs of misfortune began in that childhood bedroom transformed by my reveries into Miss Minchin's school attic.

During early adulthood, poverty was my lot, and I tried to imitate Sara's resilience. After all, she neither complained nor stopped helping those less fortunate, like my stray animals, abject souls, worthwhile charities, and lost sheep. When affluent, I delight in being able to befriend and aid those with little and, like Sara, always favour scapegoats over victors, the poor over the wealthy, the unfortunate over the blessed. Taking a note from Sara's loyalty, I'm tenacious and committed to my cohort of strange friends.

One of the toughest lessons I learned from *A Little Princess* was that weak-mindedness proliferates and dominates in groups, and that virtue attracts bullies. Despite the ultimate triumph of the human imagination in the book, its harsh realism made me aware of the destructiveness of envy and the dangers of exploitation. This awareness has made me very careful about my blindness, illusions, privilege, and power. Faced with catastrophic loss, the too-early death of my beloved mother, I found solace in remembering Sara's suffering when she lost her father. Rather than resisting grief, I took inspiration from how her darkest moments and thoughts honoured him.

I grew up sharing Sara Crewe's particular interest in stories about the French Revolution and the visions of The Book of Revelation. Even in trivial ways, such as in my passion for dolls, dresses, and food, I was like Sara, and I have carefully tended these three elements of childhood for my daughters. Who knows whether I was drawn to the little "princess" because of a pre-existing similarity or whether it was reading her which made us alike? Sara Crewe acted as an alter ego at a significant transition in my maturation. When I see a panhandler, I think of the buns devoured by the beggar girl, and I open my purse. When a lonely or misunderstood person tells me their problems, motherless four-year old Lottie comes to mind. When one of my students is slow-witted, I think of sweet Ermengarde. There is high moral ground on which to tread if we can but reach for it.

The swallows began migrating south, while the crickets and cicadas filled the September air with music. I returned to school and eagerly signed out *A Little Princess*, which I finished reading in a hurry; however, after a summer of living in and through the story in multiple plotlines from my own imagination, the end of the book hardly mattered. Narrative has such a powerful hold on us because, as Joseph Campbell writes in *The Hero's Journey*, our lives are stories in which we are the heroes. Unlike that summer long ago, the intersection of the narrative of my life with Francis Hodgson Burnett's story never ended. Stories are dreams that we awaken to find true.

Sacred Effects of Simple Things

Dorothy Nielsen

O taste and see
the subway Bible poster said

("O Taste and See" by Denise Levertov)

I am in first grade. I haul a burgundy tome to school, a collection of poetry borrowed from my parents' bookshelves. It's unwieldy, almost too heavy for my spindly arms, and I can't decipher most of the words. I use it mainly as a bench to perch on in the schoolyard during recess.

Back at home, I spend hours on the floor crouched over the book, turning over its delicate leaves, trying to make sense of the unfamiliar syntax and difficult vocabulary, searching for my favourite page with its rectangle of black print surrounded by a smooth white expanse and a one-word title centred above in blacker ink: Love. A word both easily decipherable and mysterious at the same time.

I have fallen for the concrete and abstract particularity of this artifact. I love the royally coloured cotton shell, the compact arrangement of words on the page, and the echoing places it opens in my thoughts and around my heart.

In retrospect, I interpret this literary enchantment as an augury of the poems I would publish, the PhD dissertation and the literary criticism I would write on Denise Levertov, and the decades I would teach literature and be a creative writing consultant at universities. I suspect that many people at age 64 can look back to early childhood and see themselves carrying around an object: some *thing* that comforts, delights the senses, fascinates the imagination, and foretells the directions life will take.

––––––––––

The thing about books, then, is that a book is a thing. But not just any kind of thing. Because it is an object built with and for words, a book is a curious admixture: a physical artifact that can hold the most extramundane contemplation of metaphysical realms. These objects can encase the ideas by which we live and for which we might even be willing to die. A book, then, can be a repository of a writer's or a reader's soul.

Books are also records of life phases. Dorothy Sayers wrote that "Books, you know...are like lobster shells. We surround ourselves with 'em, then we grow out of 'em, and leave 'em behind, as evidence of our earlier stages of life." Although I haven't been reading Denise Levertov's poetry and essays much over the past two decades, I keep about 20 volumes of her work close at hand, on my main bookshelf. This collection forms a carapace I shed years ago yet keep nearby as evidence of a stage in young adulthood.

A poem printed on a page, too, is a concrete thing holding ideas and ideals. At age 26, I encountered Levertov's poem "O Taste and See." This meeting was a *coup de foudre* that rewired my brain at a crucial point in my life. Neuroscientists have confirmed that reading creates new neural networks and increases the brain's white matter. My own experience suggests that reading a highly significant book or poem, by making me wrestle with new truths, not only effects minor, gradual neural changes, but might also initiate a huge developmental leap. From the vantage point of late middle age, I can think of at least seven or eight other life-changing, gobsmacking literary artifacts, a collection of Millay's poetry, the first Shakespeare play I read, Eliot's *The Waste Land*, and Dostoyevsky's *The Brothers Karamazov* notable among them.

After I read this Levertov poem in the first year of my PhD studies, I took to carrying around the volume — entitled *O Taste and See* — that held it. Here is a transcript of the page that hijacked my imagination:

The world is
not with us enough.
O taste and see

the subway Bible poster said,
meaning **The Lord**, meaning
if anything all that lives
to the imagination's tongue,

grief, mercy, language
tangerine, weather, to
breathe them, bite,
savor, chew, swallow, transform,

into our flesh our
deaths, crossing the street, plum, quince,
living in the orchard and being

hungry, and plucking
the fruit.

This poem blew my mind by compressing into a mere 63 words multiple ideas and ideals that I had been grappling with, including a poetics of direct, concrete, plain-style language, a non-materialistic philosophy of life, a psychology of healing by encounter with painful emotions, and several key Catholic concepts.

Most joltingly, the poem provided one of those conceptual shifts that happen in an instant, just as a click of a kaleidoscope rearranges the pattern; it seemed to offer a solution to a longstanding dilemma, namely, my perception of a distressing gap between the everyday physical world and the inner spiritual or imaginative realms to which I loved to flee.

At ages one, two, and three — I've been told — while my siblings tumbled together, I sat contentedly under the dining room table contemplating the world and telling myself stories. At seven, during summer vacation, I sometimes joined family and neighbourhood games late after having taken myself off alone to morning Mass a few blocks away. That was also the year I started to spend long hours in my room reading novels and novellas. One of my favourites told the story of a little prince from a tiny planet he calls Asteroid 325 who must die in this world so he can return to his home of near-continuous sunsets where he has left the one flower he loves. Like many abstract thinkers, I found the extroverted culture of contemporary North America inconvenient and disorienting, so it wasn't difficult to relate to the little prince who felt alien among the things of earth.

The flowers, stones, trees, seashells, books, the flour and sugar and butter I bake with, the physicality of the objects I love, have always held my deep attachment. But my primary orientation to things is symbolic and affective rather than instrumental, and, from a very early age, I felt compelled to shift from doing practical actions with my favourite objects to writing dreamy poetry about them. Long hours of reading, writing, and abstract thought about religion and philosophy became my welcome escapes from the physical world. However, by the time I encountered "O Taste and See," I understood that the life of householding, teaching, and mothering on which I was feeling called to embark would require a more down-to-earth relationship with the things around me, over which I tended to trip metaphorically and literally. Levertov's poem shifted my perception of this disjunction between the everyday physical plane and the captivating metaphysical realm by presenting the gritty grimy urban landscape with its subway and its fruit stands as a vital and alluring interface with the transcendent.

Reading this poem feels like participating in a ritualistic encounter with the Divine: a communion that, astonishingly, arises from a mundane walk through the urban jungle. "O Taste and See" belongs to a relatively small set of theistic religious poems that employ concrete everyday images to enter *so deeply* into the particularity of objects that *things themselves* effect union with their transcendent Creator. I would eventually have the same quasi-sacramental experience with other poems: Gerard Manley Hopkins' "The Windhover" and "Pied Beauty," which present mystical union in vivid imagery famous for capturing the "thisness" (*hacceitas*) of each thing; A. R. Ammons' sensuously particularized imagery in his "Hymn" to God; and Levertov's other poems of communion via the mundane, "Matins" and "Illustrious Ancestors." This sort of religious poem is rare because it is assertively physical and metaphysical at the same time. Even when it evokes the abstract realm, it will not turn its gaze — except fleetingly — from the literal.

Most of the famous poetic works of mystical union with God that I love are not intent on image as image. Instead, they rely on "turns" of language, also called *tropes*, such as symbols or metaphors. An image becomes the "vehicle" of meaning once the poet has "turned" away from the literal to the metaphorical or symbolic level. T.S. Eliot's *Four Quartets* captivates me with its interconnection between the physical world of time and the eternal sphere of God. Key images in *Four Quartets* move through time and then eventually are frozen in atemporal essences: for example, roses which have faded over time and collected dust are initially a concrete image; much later in the poem, the rose recurs as a more elusive symbol for God and salvation.

But it was poetry that focuses on concrete imagery which I treasured as I would seashells collected from a delightful ocean visit. During the many years I chose to exile myself from the Catholic Church to which I had been deeply drawn from an early age, works like "O Taste and See" became reminders of what I had left behind. Perhaps because of their uncanny parallels with sacramental theology, they provided for me an imaginative substitute for Holy Communion.

I read and reread Levertov's lyrical story of tasting and seeing "The Lord" (the Christian title for Jesus, Son of God, as well as for God the Father) in mundane activities and things. This poetic drawing together of the transcendent and earthly realms has distinctly sacramental overtones. Roman Catholic Eucharistic theology celebrates a physical and metaphysical interface in its mysterious belief that in Holy Communion, the bread and wine remain completely their actual selves even after having been changed into the body and blood of Jesus. Since Jesus is the incarnation of the God of Genesis, the communicant consumes both the food and drink and also God the Creator. For nearly two millennia, the Catholic Church has taught that God instituted sacramental signs using simple things, like bread and wine, which have the power to produce the sacred effects of which they are signs.

In this poem about the sacred effects of simple things, Levertov draws heavily on her Jewish and Anglican background, and she also points forward to her conversion to Roman Catholicism. "O Taste and See" opens with a quotation from Psalm 34, then goes on to present a mimetic re-enactment of taking communion at an Anglican or Roman Catholic Mass with the poet-speaker wandering through an urban landscape seeing and tasting her Creator in the subway, street, weather, and vendors' fruits. Even the everyday act of talking conjures the sweetness of mystical communion, as the words "tongue" and "language" remind me that speaking is a physical act while they allude indirectly to Jesus as the Word.

Whenever the poem might tempt me to leave the concrete plane, it pulls me back to earthly objects for an even fuller connection to God. For example, both the personification in the phrase "imagination's tongue" and the symbolic overtones of the orchard seem at first to be tropes that would turn my attention from the literal level to the neo-Romantic, Idealistic concept that what is most real is not the thing in itself but the idea of the thing. This philosophy could easily stir up my old sense of a distressing gap between the everyday world and the spiritual plane. However, the poem's entire thrust — from the first line that reverses the opening of a famous poem by Wordsworth to the last image of picking fruit — is instead an *anti*-Idealistic insistence that we access all meaning, even the most transcendent, by way of the world around us existing in space and time. Whenever I might think the poem settles into a static state, it paradoxically invites me into communion with the unchanging, unmoving, otherworldly Creator from my position *within*, not from *outside of*, mutable earthly things and time, reminding me of temporality over and over again with numerous participial constructions — "meaning," "crossing," "being," "plucking."

―――――――――

Rare poems of mystical union with the Maker by means of mundane things address the profound longing that the Psalmist expressed when he sang, "My soul thirsts for God." These poems not only deepen my understanding of this unrest but also offer a respite.

In my eyes, Levertov's "O Taste and See" exemplifies this uncommon literary trove. Though it took decades to realize, at age 26 I had stumbled upon a thing I needed badly, a page in a book on which was inscribed this unusual and precious artifact that opened a poetic portal between what had seemed like two competing spheres of existence. It kept alive my attachment to sacramental thinking until eventually I returned to the Catholic Church. It helped me to make peace between two warring parts of myself, and it led me to taste and see the wonders of everyday things.

Trees

ANNA LEE-DIEMERT

"Oh, Trees, Trees, Trees," said Lucy (though she had not been intending to
speak at all). "Oh, Trees, wake, wake, wake. Don't you remember it? Don't
you remember me? Dryads and Hamadryads, come out, come to me."

  Though there was not a breath of wind they all stirred about her. The
rustling noise of the leaves was almost like words. The nightingale stopped
singing as if to listen to it. Lucy felt that at any moment she would begin
to understand what the trees were trying to say. But the moment did not
come. The rustling died away. The nightingale resumed its song. Even in the
moonlight the wood looked more ordinary again. Yet Lucy had the feeling (as
you sometimes have when you are trying to remember a name or a date and
almost get it, but it vanishes before you really do) that she had just missed
something: as if she had spoken to the trees a split second too soon or a split
second too late, or used all the right words except one, or put in one word
that was just wrong."

(*Prince Caspian* by C.S. Lewis)

L ike Lev Grossman, in the essay that prompted mine, I grew up
thinking about *The Lion, the Witch and the Wardrobe*. It was my
favourite book for many years, and it was a book that, at a certain age,
I re-enacted at every opportunity. But if I were pressed to choose a
novel that I have thought and felt most deeply about, the less popular
Prince Caspian is the book that haunts me. I have since learned that

many people think this is the weakest of C.S. Lewis's *Narnia* series. "It's weirdly paced" is a common criticism. "The plot isn't linear. It takes forever to find out what the conflict is." And most of all, "They spend so much time just walking and talking!"

I have come to terms with the fact that I am in the minority when it comes to my love of walking — and talking, and camping — in novels. I do not have a defense for why I think reading about characters while they walk is the heart of fantasy literature, except for the passage that I chose above. Lucy Pevensie, who has been called back to Narnia after 1300 years and has hiked all day toward an unfamiliar conflict for mysterious reasons, stares up through the tree branches at night and feels a thrill of memory.

Lucy's recognition, when she looks up at the sky and puts humanoid faces to each type of tree, is weighted by 1300 years of grief. Erosion has altered the landscape she grew up in, a colonial state rules Narnia through historical revisionism, and Lucy's own family are frustrated with her insistence on staring at trees while they race toward the next plot point. It is Lucy's inability to articulate why she delays their journey that wrenched my heart — the gap between alienation and isolation that growing up creates. That gap scared me as a child, whenever stopping to drink in some scenery made me lose sight of my parents on an outing, and it still does, when my preference for wonder gives me nothing to contribute to friends' conversations about their families, aspirations, and careers.

Like Lucy walking to Aslan's Howe, I have spent days struggling to keep up with people faster and more decisive than I am, only to look outside at 2:00 a.m. and feel my mind come awake. In the works of C.S. Lewis, there are degrees of wakefulness. There is waking up when you are fatigued and half-asleep, there is the nominal "awakeness" that our work and school lives require, and there is "waking up" from winter to summer, from exams to holidays, and from the ordinary to the "dreamish wakeful" state that comes with fresh air at night, with walking alone into the woods and hearing the leaves rustle for the first time in too many years.

I do not want this to be an essay about distraction, or about hustle and productivity, or about the epidemic of mental illness that has swept like fire through my entire generation. I will only say that at the height of my effort to achieve something, to have a social role, and to reach the next plot point that might give shape to my own narrative, I suddenly lost the ability to read. The loss was instant and dramatic. In August, I flew through a large pile of novels and fell in love with each one. In October, I was assessed for lack of energy, focus or will-power, based on my lost literacy. By January, I could dimly remember what it felt like to be awake. I did what students do when they are trying to boost their minds. I downloaded apps. Made lists. And the more order I imposed, the more the forest fire burned, and the more every sentence of text blurred into nothingness as I stared at it. Especially fiction. Especially fantasy fiction.

So much of fantasy fiction is about walking. So much of *Prince Caspian* is about wandering through the dark, haunted woods toward the unfamiliar, and hoping for the divine — or intuition — to intervene. I suspect many of us never fully escape the belief that to wander into a dream-state, especially a joyful one, especially if it takes us away from a goal, is childish and irresponsible. As a student, I grew familiar with trying to coerce meanings into sentences and sentences into essays. I stopped lingering in the woods, turning my phone off, and wading in streams, because I had no social or material purpose for doing so. (What if there's broken glass? What if someone's trying to text me?) I know what it's like to be so desperate for rest on the journey that you cannot sit still and that the only way to sleep is to stop trying. I know what it feels like when every sentence has one word too many or one too few, or when every utterance is timed just a split second wrong. The grief that comes from climbing an old tree and pressing one's ear to it, only to hear bicycle bells and remember what time it is.

As children, we feel the trees bending toward us and see instinctively the shapes of faces and arms in their branches. To go outside alone at that age is terrifying, not because some animal or stranger might attack us, but because the world is so large that if we were to step into it for a second, we might never find our way back. Lucy steps through a wardrobe into Narnia and she stays there for fifteen years. She steps back the other way, and a millennium passes without her.

"Don't you remember it?" The echo of every fairy tale. Of every great novel, every imaginative experience, every ideal. Everyone who has tried to recount a dream knows the struggle of describing what mattered about it. Likewise with Narnia. We know that the landscape was once thriving with spirits, gods and fairies, and that the animals could once talk to us, but we will never be able to prove it. Telmarine soldiers have banned those haunted woods.

Lucy Pevensie is the heroine of the early *Narnia* books, but there is nothing convenient about her heroism. She is gifted, we are told, with a unique ability to see Aslan and to understand his desires, but these are frustrating abilities, not the ones she would choose for herself, not strength or beauty, judgement or power. Again and again, we see Lucy at odds with her companions, pointing at a spot in the woods, at the empty air between two trees, saying, "There. Right there! Don't you see?" For Lewis, this is a matter of religious faith, but I believe it transcends any allegorical interpretation. Rather, the book asks what we mean when we ascribe belief to anything. What does it mean when the evidence of our senses and the sense-perceptions of those closest to us are contradictory?

Lucy may well have seen something, think the others, but why can't she do the courtesy of making it visible for all? Why can't she offer proof? Why can't she *let it go*? Why must she waste everyone's time — the reader is itching for the good bits: a battle, King Miraz's defeat, the restoration of order — waffling between truth and affirmation? Why does this character drag her heels, angry and reproachful, downstream toward the battleground and away from the stars between the trees, except that to do otherwise is to be alone? Magic, so the trope goes, is a metaphor for the childish imagination, fixed in the past, hence the convention of fairy tales which justify themselves to the reader by being only a dream.

But what if, as in *The Chronicles of Narnia*, the "dreamish wakefulness" of magic is not a thing that we wake from at all, but a thing that we forget? What if the true dream world is this gray highway, the walls of the 1940s boarding school, restrictive on a scale hardly imaginable, the self-policing of the human mind? Clock in. Clock out. "It's all in *Plato*, all in *Plato*," says Professor Kirke. "Bless me, *what do they teach them in these schools?*"

I did not want to write this essay. Following my stint as an achiever, the very thought of writing, of trying to spin truth into *ideas* and then ideas into words causes a psychosomatic response that starts with a feeling of cold tension in the spine, then numbness in the arms, then a brain fog and light-headedness that leads to compulsive popping of the ears. You see, I do not know why the Pevensies returned to Narnia. Everything they do to restore Prince Caspian's right to the throne, the prince, and most definitely the Lion, could have done without them. I don't really know how the novel operates, or why its non-linear plot is so unpopular, or why Lucy's particular arc, which has nothing material to do with the title character or the usurpation of his kingship, is ultimately so vital to both. I tap my keyboard and know that I have used all the right words except one or put in one word that was just wrong. I look out the window and — wait — what am I doing here? This… is not right at all.

The lion is twitching his tail. He is waiting. He is wild and fierce and ready to blast apart the footprint of empire, to burst river gods free from their shackles to flood dams, to topple monuments, to let the trees reclaim their own.

"*Don't you remember it?*" I whisper. "*Don't you remember me?*"

IV – INTROSPECTION

Unfathomable Poetics

MATTHEW ROONEY

A t fourteen, I started playing music as a structured escape from an unstable home. Good music saved me from the bad ends that many in my high school cohort met. Growing up as a poor kid in the have-not province of Nova Scotia, I had few models of how to become an artist. The Halifax-based band April Wine made it big in the 1970s due to a misunderstood rejection letter, and they were the one exemplar. What I encountered were mediocre bands stuck in the local scene—bands who lacked that gusto, that energy, that universal expression which made music more than sound. I fixated on these three traits as essential parts of good art, and I learned to value them. I wanted to be a musician, not a piece of local colour. When my tastes turned from music to poetry, the three traits carried over. The gusto and energy came easy to me. One of the first poems I wrote during this period opens with the lines, "I sit out at Venice Beach / watching the sun cascade over / my massive sweat-glistened pectorals." Universal expression was a bit more difficult, it turned out—would you believe my pectorals are hardly visible and that I've never been to Venice Beach?

I shunned writing about where I've been and, by extension, about my own personal experiences. I justified this behaviour through a Beckettian pose of seeking truth through negation: once we remove all particulars, we are left with only fresh-caught universals flopping and struggling to survive in an otherwise-empty hellscape of our own creation. In this mode of thinking, the greater the distance between me and the concept, the closer it was to truth or universality. It was as if personal experiences were dark, deceptive voids that served as north to truth's south. Beyond pointing to how well a negative self-image marries Rationalism's long history of erasing subjectivity, I can't explain how I arrived at these ideas. I can, however, speak to how I moved beyond them.

I first encountered Elizabeth Bishop in a second-year American literature survey course at Dalhousie University. We read "The Fish," "The Moose," and "One Art." The works—particularly "One Art" and "The Fish"—troubled me because they were very clearly *good* yet had none of the gusto or energy I'd told myself were necessary. I wrote Bishop off as a poetic anomaly rather than question my convictions. The second time I encountered Elizabeth Bishop was after a poetry reading. I read my Venice Beach poem and a few others to a small group, where I met professor emeritus John Barnstead. We talked for a bit and John mentioned his involvement in the Elizabeth Bishop Society, which manages Bishop's childhood home in Great Village, Nova Scotia. John must have noticed my surprise, because he gave me a reading list. The first poem on that list was "At the Fishhouses."

Bishop's poem is set in Lockeport, a historic fishing town just south of Halifax. It opens with an image familiar from my childhood: an old man netting down by the water's edge. Bishop describes how the smell of cod evokes watery eyes, as if they are crying out to become part of the ocean again. She describes the silver fishing tools laid haphazardly yet makes them appear ordered against the wilder terrain. She then approaches the old man and offers him a cigarette (Lucky Strike, an American brand). It turns out that the old man was a friend of her grandfather. The two discuss the declining population of fish, but we also know that he's referring to the decline of fishing work and young men willing to take it on. These images and these topics are still present in rural fishing villages on the Atlantic coast. The young always leave; the old stick together and fish, because they know nothing else. Bishop's speaker observes the old man in more detail. Upon this closer inspection, however, he becomes the very image of a rural opulence. The fish scales that cover him turn to sequins that cover his clothes and his flesh. Suddenly, the man becomes a locus of Romantic, Atlantic-Canadian beauty who absorbs small bits of the sublime—the fish's iridescence. The implied aesthetic relationship between the poet and the old man has completely inverted. The move was the same that Wordsworth pulled with his old leech gatherer. But I'd grown up with these old men. Who could think of them as beautiful objects of poetry? Bishop, apparently. She'd grown up with them too. Her speaker, at least, has a grandfather of the same cloth.

The second verse paragraph is a seemingly innocuous description of the ramp the fishermen use to haul their boats to shore. Still blinded by the shimmer of the old man's vest, I pause and read this passage again. The ramp is made out of horizontal silver trees at exactly measured intervals. The silver tree trunks reminded me of the silver benches, tools, and lobster pots that the speaker mentioned earlier, but also of the sea itself which introduces the passage that itemizes the worker's tools. Silver exists on the boundaries of the natural and the technological, and it wasn't until the trees served this technological role that I realized Bishop was doing more than just describing some rural sublime—she was placing the origins of a poetic argentine age on those very shores I'd turned my back on. The intervals solidified this for me. Four-or-five-foot structures organize many of the serious—and dare I say great—poems in the Western canon. But fishing can't be a metaphor for poetry, right? The old man is a Wordsworth, in a sense, but he is also the man gathering leeches. He has an aesthetic ability that Wordsworth, I feel, rarely gives his rural figures. Either way, the ramp that goes down into the ocean that the fishermen use only *facilitates* the act. I saw this ramp—and its utility in crossing water/land boundaries—as a mental process that allows concepts to be drawn from the abstract to the concrete.

After this sestet, I raced through the rest of the poem. The last section, which makes up about half of the work, is a lyrical meditation on the Atlantic Ocean. Bishop draws attention to the depth and clarity of the water, which makes sense, then deems it unbearable to mortals, which is less comprehensible. Bishop spends the first half of the poem describing an industry that extracts mortal creatures from this same ocean, so certainly mortals can bear its elements. The poem faced me with two possible readings: 1) the sea creatures are immortal, or 2) she's not actually talking about the ocean here. Considering the earlier reference to a declining fish population, the first reading seemed unlikely. Not until the end of the poem did I discover that the Atlantic Ocean is our imaginative idea of knowledge. The fish, then, are calcified pieces of that knowledge which the old man drags into our world. Fishing is not poetry in either of these works, but both acts involve hauling concrete truths and nourishment from a realm of unfathomable, historical knowledge. Both acts also beautify those who engage with them, even if that beauty is not noticeable until a close inspection. But unlike poetry, the navigation of boundaries between the stable, concrete land and the mutable ocean is an essential part of life on the Atlantic. Fishermen like Bishop's old man subsist in these liminal spaces and are beautified by the very transgressions that force them to be static, rural, and, dare I say it, local.

I still have trouble articulating exactly how the passage shifted my understanding of poetry. I had thought that, in the service of good art, I had to avoid writing about places like Lockeport. Yet here I was faced with Bishop quietly turning an everyday piece of local colour into a near-mythical site of poetic genesis. At first, I was lost, as the essence of places I knew seemed to shift. Soon I realized that they were reaching toward their own small, local truths. The content of our identity, after all, is made of specific details, of known objects and what they can tell us. To risk a cliché unimaginable to the self I described at the beginning of this essay: the map to good art was around me all along. At the end of our conversation, John invited me to spend a weekend writing at Elizabeth Bishop House. This invitation was also part of John's reasoning for giving me homework—besides, of course, his being a professor emeritus. He wanted to prime me so that I could appreciate the deep poetic importance of that house. We planned the retreat for the middle of March 2020, but it was silently cancelled once the first few cases of COVID-19 emerged in the country. I regret not visiting that house in Great Village. I regret that I had closed myself off to the beauty of my home province until it was too late for me to freely experience it.

A few months into the pandemic I moved to Newfoundland. One year later, I moved again to Ontario, where I've lived landlocked for the last three years. Reading "At the Fishhouses" does far more than make me appreciate Bishop's connection to Atlantic Canada. The poem has become an anchor that continues to connect me with the province that gave me shape. Time away from Nova Scotia has made it more and more evident that I am a salt-water creature. I am of the local colour—an uncommon expression of it, perhaps, but a complementary one nonetheless. The Atlantic's briny stink has followed me and has, despite my reticence, started wrinkling the pages of my own writing. The ocean has become a fixed part of my identity in a dry and unfamiliar land. I swell with pride when people recognize where I'm from—say, from the way my "aunts" emphasize the u and sound more like "haunt" than "ant." Bishop must have felt the same way. She was taken in by her maternal grandparents in Nova Scotia at the age of five, after her mother was institutionalized. Her father had already died four years earlier. Though Bishop lived in the province for only two years, she wrote about Nova Scotia for her entire literary career. The province might have served Bishop as a place of stability in her unstable childhood. Perhaps I am projecting too much.

Critics accuse Bishop of hiding or decentering herself in her works. Yes, she is an obscure presence compared to Wordsworth's egotistical sublime. Obscurity is not obfuscation, however. In a letter to Robert Lowell, Bishop questions his description of a Maine town they'd visited together. She accuses him of lying to serve some aesthetic end. She can't do that. This honesty, I think, is the virtue of Bishop's poetry, and it is worth more than any amount of gusto, energy, or universal expression. These brief moments where art captures reality are lighthouses in a fog-filled world. Without "At the Fishhouses" and its play between poetry and fishing, land and water, locality and knowledge, I would still be surrounded by the fog of my own negations. Knowledge comes not from deceptions, denials, or language games. Knowledge comes from the willingness to throw small truths back into their native waters. Throw enough in and one might come back large and sparkling. Throw enough of those larger truths back and eventually, with hope and patience, something unfathomable might momentarily break the surface.

That Inward Eye

JACQUELINE CHATEAUVERT

For oft, when on my couch I lie
In vacant or in pensive mood,
They flash upon that inward eye
Which is the bliss of solitude.

("I Wandered Lonely as a Cloud" by William Wordsworth)

When I was a ten-year-old child in post-war England, I had the privilege of being taught English by a very insightful teacher. As I prepared for my 11+ exam, which would direct my future education, Miss Gertrude Foster took a special interest in me. She seemed very old but was probably about 60, which would have meant she was a Victorian, as were my grandparents. Now, in my 80th year, I'm astonished to think that she may well have been able to remember Queen Victoria's funeral in 1901. The recent death of Her Majesty Queen Elizabeth reminded me of this time as it was this late Queen's Coronation year of which I write.

At the country school I attended, English was taught in three parts, and each week we had a double period for Literature, and another double period devoted to oral English when we learned how to recite, sometimes performing short plays or memorable speeches — all this to imbue us with confidence to speak in front of people. Grammar (thankfully) was only one period per week, but, in hindsight, should perhaps have been more. During Oral English, we were required to learn and recite for the class a particular poem or speech, and choice could be made from anything covered in class, from Milton to Blake, Shakespeare to Tennyson, Wordsworth to Shelley, Dickinson to Yeats, and many others. It fell to my lot to learn and recite William Wordsworth's "I Wandered Lonely as a Cloud," commonly known as "Daffodils." I diligently learned the entire poem by heart — driving my family nuts in the process, my sister even declaring that she had come to loathe daffodils — as I prepared to deliver this masterpiece to the class.

In later years, I considered that Wordsworth's poem had likely been learned by many children schooled under the English system, despite the vast majority of them never having laid eyes on daffodils. I was fortunate enough to have seen the flowers of which Wordsworth wrote in full bloom along the shores of Lake Windermere close to where he lived. But I came to appreciate that this poem is not just about flowers, and that special insight has forever coloured my perception of self.

A few days prior to the scheduled recitation, Miss Foster would meet with each student to discuss the piece to be performed and offer analysis and encouragement to look deeper into the meaning of what was to be recited. Thanks to her insight, I came to appreciate that the true message had little to do with daffodils. The flowers were merely metaphors for the events of life. The words that made the most impact and remain with me to this day are from the last stanza:

> For oft, when on my couch I lie
> In vacant or in pensive mood,
> They flash upon that inward eye
> Which is the bliss of solitude;
> And then my heart with pleasure fills,
> And dances with the daffodils.

The key phrase here is "that inward eye / Which is the bliss of solitude." At ten, I was not much concerned with solitude or bliss. "Rock 'n Roll" had not yet arrived, but there were film stars and singers to go gaga over, although contact with popular media was sparse — no TV for a start. Newspapers then, of which there were many, had multiple pages and sections, and were mines of information about everything, including stars of stage and screen. However, Miss Foster opened a new door for me when she stated that despite friends, family, lovers (although her description only considered married love), and my own future children, I would live my entire life inside my own head.

Although my true understanding of what that meant took some time to mature, throughout the years since, I have repeatedly recalled those lines of poetry and the first time I said the words "bliss of solitude." The beauty of solitude is that one can daydream about events in the past that have been the source of pleasure, pain, trepidation, elation, bliss and even fear — a whole lifetime in one's own head. One can also plan future events. In a similar manner, we can enjoy quiet thoughts of how to re-decorate a room, write a poem, buy a new outfit, plan a vacation; anything that catches and engages the imagination is frequently best achieved in solitude. I am also reminded of the release of tension brought by confession and find that solitary thought about events which might have not gone as planned, or could have been different, is helpful for growing in the future and healing in the present.

A few years back, I had the opportunity and privilege to attend Brescia University as a mature student. When asked to present a poem in much the same way as I had in 1953, I chose "Daffodils." Before even beginning, I showed the class several pictures of the Lake District with daffodils blooming beside Lake Windermere. I asked my fellow students to close their eyes while I recited, and try to think about the words and be carried along by their own visual images. When the poem was finished, I asked them if they knew what was meant by "the bliss of solitude," but sadly not all had considered either "bliss" or "solitude" in their lives to that point. I was given a good mark for my presentation, and, interestingly enough, a few years later, one of my fellow students told me that they had been enjoying an internal reverie when suddenly the phrase "bliss of solitude" made absolute sense. It does not follow that Miss Foster's interpretation of Wordsworth is the "right" one or that everyone will agree with her view, but her vision of his meaning has been of major importance in my life.

During the pandemic, people around the world had their own forms of solitude to deal with. And for myself — I have lived alone for 23 years — poetry and reading in general have been sources of great solace when social contact was curtailed. Long walks thinking about and enjoying nature have given meaning to solitude. I know that many people found the trials of the Covid lockdown overwhelming, but I came through unscathed and even perhaps more emotionally secure than ever. At times of loneliness, personal loss, and fear, I have silently thanked Miss Foster as a very wise woman and wished that I could have the opportunity to tell her what a difference she made to one little girl. That little girl passed her 11+, one of only four from the school, and enjoyed a first-class education, and much later, she passed the importance of solitude along to her daughters, grandson, and now great-granddaughter, who all have come to know the importance of living inside one's own head.

Creating Monsters Within

ALICIA MOORE

The characters and larger society of Chris Wooding's *The Haunting of Alaizbel Cray* take the products of their nightmares and literally turn them into monsters, the "wych-kin." They twist feelings of guilt, hate, shame, and any other parts of themselves they dislike, and create monsters to torture themselves, all while remaining completely unaware of their hand in their own torment and destruction.

I read *The Haunting of Alaizabel Cray* for the first time when I was in grade 10. I read the back, but the synopsis gave no indication of the effect the novel would have on me. The description on the back cover should have been a clue — "a post-goth masterpiece about a shattered society and all the evil that dwells within" — but I still expected only literal monsters. I was unprepared for the human darkness that would be revealed at the end, monsters much more terrifying than the ones the protagonists spend the book fighting.

Near the final chapter, one particular passage captures the concept Dr Pyke, the main antagonist, was desperate to impress upon the protagonist, Nathaniel. Dr. Pyke attempts to save humanity from its self-destructive compulsion to create monsters by providing citizens with new, terrible Gods to believe in. He comes across as quite the madman for much of the novel, and yet, when given the chance to explain himself, he makes terrifying sense. Dr Pyke rants about the twisted way in which the people around him give life to their nightmares without realizing it. They take all the things they dislike about themselves, the feelings of guilt, hate, and shame, and fashion monsters to chase and torment them in their waking life, rather than facing themselves. Dr. Pyke doesn't see himself as a monster, but he possesses the same flaw he imputes to the rest of humanity: blaming external monsters for personal shortcomings he lacks the maturity to face. As I wrestled to understand that concept, the words seemed to grow roots and dig themselves deeper and deeper into my brain.

Assuming novels written for teens address only superficial themes, people often dismiss Young Adult literature. However, larger truths and meanings reside in "teen" books like *The Haunting of Alaizabel Cray* that everyone would benefit from reflecting on. It was fortuitous to have read this book, and those specific lines, during such an important stage in my life. From this book, and others like it that followed, I learned to not simply accept the world at face value. Around the time I read the book, my mother told me that some "flaws" people point out in others are actually things that they dislike in themselves and are not ready, or willing, to face. Everyone has flaws, but we have the power to choose what to do about them. I could choose to reject or accept these false flaws, I could choose to face my own flaws, and others could choose to throw their flaws outside of themselves, pretending they do not belong to them. While I did struggle to not accept blame for things that were not my fault or were outside my power to control, this book, and the last few chapters in particular, set me up to challenge the blame and to see opportunities for choice. I could understand why someone would want to avoid mental distress or cognitive dissonance by casting their monsters outside of themselves. The book and that highly influential passage urged me to examine things differently, to wonder *why* something or someone is the way it is, rather than simply accepting things at face value.

Chris Wooding's novel made me appreciate the line "God made man sufficient to stand, but free to fall" from *Paradise Lost* that led me to write an essay on free will versus predestination during university. I was interested in why people would be so eager to give away control: to avoid responsibility, to evade tough choices. I had seen family members with cancer, people who desperately sought control over a relentless disease. It was so easy to say it was "God's Plan," but I didn't want to accept that answer. Disease is so much more complex, but who wants to look at their life and realize that their choices, or the choices of a parent or employer, brought them to a crisis? Attributing unexpected events to predestination is logically similar to projecting personal faults onto external monsters. Predestination, a large and mysterious force supposedly shaping our lives, alleviates the pressure of personal responsibility. In Chris Wooding's fictional world, when superhuman forces appear to drive events, human agency lurks in the background. It becomes clear that seemingly transcendental, driving forces are born of human hands. It was free will all along, hiding behind a mask of predestination.

Psychology tells us that past experiences influence the way we interpret new ones. Faced with troubling situations, we latch onto that childish cognitive bias that resists personal responsibility and projects blame outside ourselves. Once we start looking inwards, and, by extension, imagine the inner workings of other people, there is no going back.

I had a friend in high school who seemed to thrive on conflict and often picked fights with me. Becoming reactive in those situations felt inevitable. It was years into our friendship, after reading this book, that I came to realize she was likely trying to externally process some internal frustration that she was not mature enough to tackle. There came a moment when I realized I could choose not to fight. I told her I would talk to her again when she was calm. She was livid, but the boundary needed to be set. That choice gave me my power back and left her to deal with her "monster" rather than unleashing it for me to deal with. There is power in looking inward, in choosing the path we need to follow to look after ourselves. It also better prepares us to fight or manage the monsters others have let out into the world. All of our actions involve choice, even when they seem automatic. To a great extent, we shape our own experiences. Yes, external forces constrain our choices, and we can blame those outside influences — or can we? We choose how we respond to all events, even those that appear to decide our destinies. We create our own monsters. We give them their power.

It is tough to come to terms with the darkness or monsters inside us. It's even tougher to realize those monsters weren't put there by someone else. You may want to blame your life experiences and the people around you for internal darkness or monsters, but it is not that simple. You created that monster, and it remains with you with your blessing. Pushing your monsters outside of yourself, as the characters of the novel have been doing, may provide a measure of temporary relief, but it only creates new problems — the monsters must be faced before they turn back and consume you. Dr Pyke seems like a madman for saying we need monsters because we don't want to blame ourselves, but he is right. Digging deep into ourselves is mentally and emotionally straining. It was hard for me to internalize this concept, but the effort was beneficial. I am responsible for my actions and experiences, and for how I think about people, things, and situations. Blaming an external "monster" prevents me from taking effective steps to change my experience.

Recognizing that we all grapple with inner monsters informed my development of compassion through those formative teenage years and beyond. No one is purely "good" or "bad." Each individual is a tapestry of choices. As we wrestle with our identities and objectives, our inner monsters exert varying degrees of influence over our day-to-day lives. Gaining insight into human thought processes and their defining factors has not only strengthened my day-to-day relationships, but also helped me create realistic characters in my writing. All people, fictional and non-fictional, are products of their choices. As a writer, I make choices for my characters — although some find ways of escaping me and writing their own stories. Writers invent monsters for their characters, and, by proxy, for their readers, to face. We may not engender new gods, but we offer readers a safe space to wrestle with their monsters so they may recognize them and eventually defeat them.

Seeking Wonder and Awareness

D'ARCY ALLEN

It was a chilly February afternoon on campus when a dear friend of mine asked me what my favourite book was. As it happens, she asked a month too soon. It was a simple and perfectly reasonable question to ask someone who a) was a university student working towards a degree in English literature and b) would consistently introduce herself as someone who had loved to read since she was a little girl. However, that winter, I felt as though reading had lost its magic. The only answer I could muster was, "I don't think I have one."

I suppose university is to blame for that loss of passion; I chose English as my major. Don't get me wrong: I couldn't see myself studying any other subject, and my professors provided me with valuable insights into works of literature I would never have read otherwise. I appreciate what I gained during my time at university, but that sense of joy — in reading for pleasure rather than for homework — did dwindle over the years. As a student, I rarely had the time I needed to *really read* the book. Any key passages I did skim were through an analytical sieve I gradually developed in hopes of finding a speck of the golden nugget that is "meaning" or "relevance." Any time I did encounter such a golden nugget, I set it aside delicately for inclusion in my next essay.

You may be wondering why I even remember that mid-February conversation. The reason is, in another month, we would be in the midst of a global pandemic. That afternoon, spent chatting and shooting pool in the student lounge with my friend, was one of my last normal interactions before everything changed.

I had always enjoyed reading fantasy novels, like the *Harry Potter* books, which have held a special place in my heart since I was thirteen, and I told my friend as much, but she wanted just one favourite book. I felt I should pick something sophisticated and regarded as *great literature* — whatever that means — something that not only had a good plot and characters, but also a unique style of writing, instead of something I enjoyed reading as a teenager. While I stood by the *Harry Potter* series as my tentative answer, I also felt pressed to undertake a grand, lifelong search for a single novel I could claim as my favourite. I feared that I would never rediscover the joy of reading an incredible story for the first time and losing myself in the pages. That changed when I stumbled across Peter S. Beagle's *The Last Unicorn*.

Funnily enough, I almost didn't read the book. Initially, my intention was to satisfy my lifelong desire to travel by enrolling in a summer course that included a trip abroad. However, as the deadline crept closer, a wave of anxiety overtook me and I chickened out. Instead, I opted for a fantasy literature course, and the syllabus happened to include Beagle's novel. About a week before the world shut down, the class was assigned a short paper on *The Last Unicorn*. Drowning in assignments, I was tempted to find a summary of the novel online and throw an essay together as quickly as possible. Fortunately, I decided to read a little before bed, since a small optimistic voice in my head whispered, "This could be the book you've been looking for — your favourite." There was also a more cynical voice, which chortled, "Like that's going to happen. But we'll read it anyway."

It's difficult for me to explain exactly where this cynicism came from. Perhaps it was a combination of the lack of joy I felt in reading book after book for assignments, and the scepticism I felt towards the whimsical title of Beagle's novel. They say don't judge a book by its cover — an overused English idiom, I know — but even though I kept an open mind, I still had some doubts about what I was about to read, believing I would be able to predict the plot based solely on the title and genre of the novel.

No words can adequately express how overjoyed I am that I

stopped and read this book, but I'll do my best. The book awakened my sense of wonder.

The plot appealed to me right away: a unicorn learns that she may be the last of her kind and decides to leave her forest home in search of her mystical brethren. But what really captured my attention was Beagle's writing. I hadn't expected humour, but his dialogue is equal parts charming and funny, his prose simple yet poetic. Beagle's words hold weight and depth, such that even the most ethereal descriptions feel tangible and intimate. I could no longer spend time in the natural world without recalling some detail from his story: wisps of white cirrus clouds resembling the mane of the unicorn, or the crimson sun sinking toward the horizon and looming over the land like the fearsome Red Bull. Even the seasons changing around me became intertwined with the passage of time in Beagle's world. As that chilly February melted into March, I couldn't help but muse on the many characters stuck in particular seasons of their lives, accepting their circumstances or desperately trying to change them.

Not only was I delighted by the colourful cast of whimsical characters; I also appreciated their metafictional awareness. The characters are fully aware that they are in a fairy tale, and that knowledge guides their actions. Dreams and desires, fears and sorrows, the presence of mortality and the search for identity plague the humans of the story. Beagle states that unicorns can feel sorrow, but they are so disconnected from the lives of mortals that they cannot comprehend regret. Like the unicorn, I could feel the weight of the humans' sorrow. Unlike the unicorn, who is immortal and does not know regret, I greatly empathized with the human characters: a magician who fears he will never master his magic, a woman in a loveless relationship who feels she has wasted her golden years, an old tyrannical king so unsatisfied with the world he desperately searches for something that will bring him happiness. All these characters could easily fit into fantasy tropes, but the choices they make, for better or for worse, break predictable patterns, turning the story on its head and giving characters a little more agency. Even though these are fictional characters in a fantasy realm, the realism of their human nature keeps the story grounded; many of their troubles reflect some of my deepest fears, or ones I will face one day.

There are countless passages from *The Last Unicorn* that I enjoy and can recite from memory, but my favourite is from an encounter between the unicorn and Schmendrick the Magician — a kind-hearted, albeit clumsy wizard, with the funniest character name I've ever come across. After being captured and exhibited in a witch's travelling circus, the unicorn learns that humans can no longer recognize her as a unicorn, and instead mistake her for a white mare. Schmendrick is one of the few characters in this story who can see without the aid of illusion and who knows the unicorn for what she is. Schmendrick claims that he knows and understands how the unicorn is misjudged, and how she must view him as clownish or untrustworthy, an enchantment to which he must submit. He tells her that her magical nature will disappear once she's free, that people are never what they seem and even more rarely what they dream, and that misunderstanding is also a kind of enchantment. Schmendrick also tells her that in ancient songs and stories unicorns can tell the difference between false and true, between laughter and sorrow.

The idea that people are neither what they seem nor what they dream arrested me during my struggle with depression and sense of lost identity. Disheartened by the realization that my self-perceptions would always be obscured by others' biased opinions, I had forsaken my belief in absolute truth. Schmendrick seemed to speak directly to my inner turmoil. This scene, like this whole novel, candidly acknowledges sorrow and regret. However, Beagle balances that bitter realism with hope. He offered the comfort I needed to hear. There is so much more to you than what other people see.

From then on, I not only trusted Schmendrick as a character, but Beagle as an author. I gladly continued the journey with these characters, eagerly reading page after page. My newfound sense of wonder followed me beyond the novel's conclusion and filled me with creative energy. *The Last Unicorn* inspired me to indulge in artistic pursuits, from sketching the unicorn to revisiting my old passion for writing and dreaming up new stories. I had not only found an author I admired, but a viable contender for my long-sought "favourite book." Beagle, Schmendrick, the Unicorn and all of the wonderful characters revived my love of reading and writing, a passion that had nearly been crushed under academic pressure. This book came into my life exactly at the right time, and I'm grateful.

Encoded Enigmas of the Salt Cellar

BRIAN DIEMERT

In a flash she saw her picture, and thought, Yes, I shall put the tree further in the middle; then I shall avoid that awkward space. That's what I shall do. That's what has been puzzling me. She took up the salt cellar and put it down again on a flower in the pattern in the table-cloth, so as to remind herself to move the tree.

(*To the Lighthouse* by Virginia Woolf)

I am without a reasonably sized pepper mill. Ours stands tall, dwarfing the dining table's accoutrements, a veritable Red Wood on an earthen plane (and it is made of red wood), its days numbered like all things in this absurd and mortal realm where a salt cellar converses with a butter dish (already twice replaced—though we fondly remember its kin). Shattered! A careless gesture (good title, that) and oblivion. The Big Sleep, Time After Time, Life After Life. It's happening again. The half-remembered books burble into the mouth (without acidity, if properly digested); the absurdity of the distraction, the fascination of the abomination (but the orange and black spines add so much to a room); the organizational key known only to me and the penguins.

They say everyone has a novel inside them. "And that's where it should stay!" the voice says. And so it should, for the private confidences of young men, as Fitzgerald suggested, are usually lies. Maybe novels reside in us, but whose novels? The shelves creak and bow under unread books; not all are novels but some are. It's also novels we *have* read that creak and bow within the bookshelf and us. Parts, scenes, and lines leak into memory. Sparkling passages illuminate unbidden thought, but excite envy — "What is the meaning of life? That was all — a simple question; one that tended to close in on one with years. The great revelation had never come. The great revelation perhaps never did come. Instead, there were little daily miracles, illuminations, matches struck unexpectedly in the dark; here was one." I marveled when I first read *To the Lighthouse*; the impression the dinner scene left on me — indelible (or do I just remember it that way?). Could that scene have changed my sense of the real or did it just confirm an intuition? Beneath the mundane talk and materiality of the scene, the tinnitus and hum of inner lives overwhelmed the food (as it often does). The shifting light, the candles, the changing courses, the conversation, and the lost broach — they are all real, but every interaction occurs thickly. How different from Joyce's dinner in *The Dead*, where social concerns dominate, and thoughts and feelings are inferred. I've read *To the Lighthouse* many times now, my admiration, oscillating waves, iambic measures through time. I've since understood Woolf's aims. In high school, I hadn't read "Modern Fiction," "A Sketch of the Past," or any of Virginia Woolf's other novels. I only wondered why anyone would be afraid of her. Now, those things are the backdrop to lectures and the scenery of discussion, an effort to explain what can probably only be felt. Still, I remember that first encounter, and then my disappointment at Mrs. Ramsay's death and the survival of her self-absorbed husband — demonstrating loss and injustice. There's a lesson.

How did Woolf do it? The boldness of the question — "What is the meaning of life?" — in a novel no less! So grand, so sententious! Would I smirk at it now, to come across such a question, unless perhaps a child asked it, interrupting grown-up conversation — "Oh, that's so cute." It was a child who asked Whitman in another poem, "What is the grass?", but Whitman turned to metaphor; no doubt leaving the tot confused. Perhaps it was cutlery or the placement of the salt or pepper that gave Woolf the idea, the permission, so that Lily Briscoe could have her vision.

Again, the mute cutlery, like the stars, silently gleams its revelations in the code of passing shadows that dull the shine until the next chromium flash. Revealing what? A smudge, a crumb of hardened something barnacularly clinging despite the dishwasher's jets and its concentrated chemicals? Is there permanence then after all or is there only the cyclic change of filth drained away to return eternally—the seasonal return of birds or ants or household vermin. The cats are too old now to fulfill their predatory roles—elder dowagers reproachful in their enforced sterility. A younger tribe is needed, and now! Rats and mice proliferate. Mechanical devices (mousetraps) are employed when organic and animate beings fail. But I was going to break in with a tale of buried stories: anthropomorphized naval vessels, talking dinnerware, the inspirations gained from tedious conversations over beautiful soup and well-placed flatware. (I feel a song coming on.) It says, however many books you cram inside, there will always be more outside bowing and cracking the shelves. You lose. You are lost. The paper rots, the glue grows brittle, the spines crack; eventually, nothing beside remains. I stole that phrase too. How can I help it—my head so full of dreams, stuffed with straw, maybe just full of goop, which rhymes with my earlier image of soup, but only the most strained of metaphors would link them productively, which we have not got—productive linkage, that is. So loss is transformation, is change, is loss, a passing after all, and a box dropped at a thrift shop.

After the mousse, the fruit and cheese board, after the soporific stuffing we've done to ourselves and the muttered burpings of "never again," the table is cleared and set anew for the 8:00 pm serving, the 10:00 pm serving, or perhaps the next day's breakfast cautiously promising some sort of dawn, hot coffee, orange juice, bacon, glistening jam on toast, bacon, runny eggs, and pastures new—another day, for now. Yet, impossible to describe it all. The real is too deep and wide, spilling "this moment in June," vulnerable and fragile, already in the scythe's arc. I grow old, I grow old—such self-pitying tripe (but that's the point!). Our children are grown, moved out; we tire each other with asking, "Have you heard from the kids today?" We get seniors' discounts (and, worse, don't even have to ask!). There are more books in this room than

I can possibly read, will ever read, in many lifetimes. There are others, not yet born, waiting to get in. How many lifetimes can there be? I have to choose, and choosing won't stop until choice is gone.

I recently read that the thing we decide most often in a day is what to put in our mouths—a permanent oral fixation, an affliction? From fingers and nipples in infancy to forks and spoons; bitten nails to tandoori masala; there's a map from one space to another, marks on the doorframe chart our growth and the conversion of nutrients into cells. What we put in our mouth—the servicing of the physical being, maybe the smallest portion of all that we think we are. The rest resides under the salt cellar constellated into private communication, encoded enigmas, messages that our task is to read.

V – DISCOVERY

Intimologies

SHELLY HARDER

In the spring of 2019, I went to Dublin for the 80th anniversary of the publication of James Joyce's *Finnegans Wake*. I was curious. I'd skimmed the tip of my nose through a few fragments, out of which I'd got almost nothing, other than the odd whiff of thrill, a brief maddening that abruptly vanished. It wasn't easy going, to put it mildly. And what's worse, the text mocks you, promising both that its intricate obscurities will occupy scholars for ages and that any keen schoolkid could tell what's going on.

That weekend, I encountered a project whose aim is to record *Finnegans Wake*, read around the world by people with varying degrees of familiarity with that infamously unreadable book. The method was simple: choose a piece of music (preferably instrumental) that matters to you, and, while listening to it, take a page given to you and read it aloud, without prior preparation. Don't think about the mic. Don't worry about the mangled wall of neologism, multi-language mishmash, tricksy non-syntactic sprawl of verbal nubs and appendages. Just let the music string your tongue across the lines.

To Stevie Ray Vaughan's tender and virtuosic rendition of "Little Wing," I set off across a page studded with hazards. But stilted nerves slowly gave way to fun as I found myself launched into an exhilarating tumble along lines that proffered the occasional glimmer of denotative sense within a wash of unnamed, unnameable sensation — the underbelly of dream, raw stranger.

I translate poorly that elation. But it propelled me from Sweny's, a pharmacy immortalised in Joyce's more infamous but significantly less unreadable *Ulysses*, and into a corner of Kennedy's, a comfortable pub panelled in dark wood, where I continued to tear syllables off the page in an uncomprehending flurry.

The next day, I slunk into the plush dust of a secluded establishment near the quays. The afternoon was murky, chilled. The previous night's surfeit had dissipated, changed, upon waking, into a slick surface that offered no grip as the minutes skidded, swerved, slid. I sipped a pot of over-steeped tea and fidgeted. *What's the etymology of origin?* The question crawled through a narrow crevice in the tenacious blank. Absently, I picked up my phone.

Sometimes, I wonder if anything comes of those long spaces composed of a wash of half-impressions, which leave only patchy sketches insinuating that something must have happened, and someone (me?) might have been there. But who knows what intricate operations — the organization of dominoes, gears, balls, ramps into a precisely calibrated chain reaction machine — might occur in the belly of that thing called a body, while its surface quakes?

That "origin" has a history is an obvious fact I'd never noticed. That words in general have histories is a fact of which I was peripherally aware. That the lives of words, strewn across millennia of palates and pages, might cluster around the contours of a life unable to grip its own dimensions was a possibility in which I shivered.

Desire. Play. Rage. Hunger. Frantic, I typed, digging into dubious histories, the tangled roots and branchings of words that spiralled into one another, a snarl of hypotheses, startling overlaps, unknown origins. And out of this clutter, I felt myself beginning to say something I hadn't known to say, that I hadn't known I could say. A story, my story, that wasn't a story, any story — for a story requires some solidity, and my infrastructure was in an equilibrium of carefully maintained collapse.

I'll step a little further back, it might be helpful. Sometimes, a story about clipping your toenails requires a history of the foundry. What I mean to say is, I'd been born into a severely insular religious group, solely rural. That life fit poorly, and at eighteen I abandoned one world for another. Much harder than relocation of body was the relocation of mind. To find new forms of life, I severed myself. Determined to acquire life on different terms, I lost the ability to make much sense to myself. I could obtain no grammar of thought that would make intelligible an existence on both sides of that divide. Sometimes, I'd howl *why?* into the night, but headlights on the highway proffered nothing.

That afternoon, as I sprinted around the internet, searching jagged sketches of grief, longing, violence, I wasn't thinking about the previous night's adventure. Later, I remembered that the *Wake* gives a name to the collision of its ruthless excavation of the personal and its minute survey of historical and cultural ground. "Intimologies" — etymologies, intimate ologies, the personal parsed through the vastness of a world authored by no one and everyone. The second chapter announces the name of its protagonist, Here Comes Everybody, a structuring ploy that fails and persists, for "everybody" is, among other things, a Viking invader, a father and husband whose relations to his family are constituted by severe power differentials. Yet, his form is a nexus of the world that's been and is, history incarnate, unavoidable — shared shape there's no reprieve from coping with.

Lengthier acquaintance with *Finnegans Wake* has made it, if anything, more unreadable, and while that first thrill of meeting has ebbed and flowed, its beautiful, vexing, taxing pages remain an instigation that won't quite leave me alone. In place of authenticity — memory stamped and authorised by that veracious (voracious?) arbitrator, the self who can verify, establish the rights, the wrongs, the significations — I met in it an inconclusive process of collaboration with dimensions that evade, exceed formulation, but a tracery of which can be cobbled, if in negative relief only.

At that juncture of baffling structures and visceral swamp — unowned, unanticipated, inexorable — might reverberate the impish shape of some tense, rich nowhere. A saying that unsays, tangles with unknowns, both known and unknown. That to be is to be scraped and brushed by an architecture intimate as your own tongue but formed from without the precincts of self. All this has been said often enough, and better. But falling into the *Wake* made it real for me, and I found myself able in that moment to write and to feel it matter. Relieved of the requirement for language to operate representationally, to function as a good and reliable copier of facts (in whose slipperiness and absence I'd been floundering) integrated fluently into justified and authoritative evaluations, I found space in which to play.

Following those days in Dublin, I spent a year tangled up in *Finnegans Wake*. And I continued intermittently to cultivate, hack at, explode, compress the piece I'd begun that gloomy afternoon. Slowly, it unfurled the sort of sense that seems to require that something happen in your gut as much as in your brain. One of the best-known features of the *Wake* is its self-consuming, ouroboric structure, its final sentence beginning its first, in a sprawling circle of mediated immediacy, a potent simultaneity of centripetal and centrifugal force. And it seemed to me that what I could have to say would always find itself already to have been said and to be unsayable. In traversing the woozy point of constellation between past and future, a.k.a. *the present*, no truth, no progression, no movement. You can only come, over and over, to where you cannot but be, your most necessary impossibility, which is everyone's, and no one's. Here was an adventure along which I'd never know just what I might find.

Perhaps it's impossible to live without some structuring myth. I've relished these lavish contradictions, constructed of that flimsiest of dreams, words, and their unravelling. Perhaps nonsense is preservation of something feasible in the face of sense that crushes. Words whirl, the clinging of life to its bones. And sometimes, I listen to "Little Wing," and the hint of a garbled tangle of syllable shimmers on the edges of each note, and something curls in my gut that is the haunting of history, that vastness into which my little life floats.

Double-Thinking the Past

Allison Pieterman

"What shall it be this time?" he said, still with the same faint suggestion of irony. "To the confusion of the Thought Police? To the death of Big Brother? To humanity? To the future?"

"To the past," said Winston.

"The past is more important," agreed O'Brien gravely.

(*1984* by George Orwell)

It's safe to say that *1984* has changed many lives. George Orwell wrote it to warn people about what would happen if Russia took over the world: about what would happen if we let communism, actual communism, creep into our society. While Orwell wrote this book to change minds, *1984* never really altered my thoughts on the government or communism or Russia. Instead, the novel pushed me up against the reality of history, and I found myself face to face with the ever-present truth of the past rather than the dangers of the present. The book made me realize that the past is both always changing and yet always the same. Most importantly, Orwell showed me how significant the past is.

And here's the thing: I study history. I talk and read about the past daily, but none of my research or classes on historiography ever made me face the reality and importance of history as this book of fiction did. More than any class ever did and more than any ever will, *1984* taught me why history matters.

In the book, George Orwell coins the term "double-think": believing something is true while knowing it is false. In section 2.3, O'Brien holds up four fingers and asks Winston how many he is holding up. Winston answers, "four." While still holding four fingers, O'Brien asks Winston what would happen if the Party said he was holding five. Would he still be holding four fingers, or five? Again, Winston insists O'Brien is holding up four fingers. O'Brien asks Winston again and again how many fingers he is holding up until Winston finally believes that O'Brien is truly holding up five fingers. Winston knows that O'Brien is holding up four fingers, but because the Party has told him five, he believes that there are five.

Another principle of the book is that there is always a war, and this war is always changing. At the beginning of the book, the war is with Eastasia. Halfway through the book, the enemy changes to Eurasia, and Big Brother instructs the population that the war has always been with Eurasia. The population knows that yesterday they were fighting Eastasia, but they also believe they have always been fighting Eurasia. This is double-think in action, and now it has changed history. The changing of the past to suit the Party's needs, Winston's job, is yet another common theme. Essentially a time-changing journalist, Winston must dive into old journals and newspapers and edit the past.

In real life, history is changeable and stubborn, a double-think in real time — two completely opposing ideas, both true. Throughout my studies, I've noticed that history easily changes depending on whose perspective you read. If you look at the slave trade through British-biased history, Britain conquered parts of Africa and collected resources for gain. If you examine the same series of events from an African perspective, white people took Africans from their homelands, sold them across the ocean, and forced them to work without compensation. Depending on what our teachers taught us as children, our view of history will differ radically from that of someone with a different background.

History can even be warped and changed to fit a political opinion.

Take those who deny the Holocaust. They completely ignore actual testimonies and point to small, hidden facts completely removed from their historical and political contexts. History changes depending how you look at it. In *1984*, O'Brien brags that the Party controls the people's minds: "We, the Party, control all records and we control all memories. Then we control the past, do we not?" Orwell's message is obvious — collective memory is changeable, as is history. If someone were to convince the entire population that the Acadian expulsion never happened, what we call history will have changed.

Paradoxically, factual history is still immutable. History stands still. It is always unchangeable. No matter how many primary sources are deleted, no matter how many survivors pass away or how many people ignore the facts, what has actually happened never changes. You could convince the whole world that Acadia and the struggles of the Acadian people never existed. This wouldn't change the fact that Acadian people lived and suffered in Canadian history.

In *1984*, one of Winston's biggest doubts about the Party concerns a scandal around three men: Jones, Aaronson, and Rutherford. The Party accuses them of conspiring with enemies. However, Winston finds a photograph of the three men overseas at the time of the supposed conspiracy. If Winston presented it to the Party, this evidence would exonerate all three men. The Ministry of Love eventually destroys this photograph, and then convinces Winston, under torture, that the three men are indeed guilty of conspiracy. O'Brien even tells Winston that Jones, Aaronson, and Rutherford have all confessed to those crimes that they never committed. Even if the Party destroyed every document that proved their innocence, that destruction would not change the actual past. Destroying all photographic evidence of an event or discounting survivors' testimonies of events cannot alter the past. People denying the Holocaust can never change the fact that the Holocaust happened. So, even if the past is mouldable and changeable, it is still immutable. It still stands unchanged even if it is changing. This is the essence of modern double-think.

Another principle that *1984* stresses is the importance of the past in shaping future and current events. In section 2.8, O'Brien and

Winston meet to discuss the Brotherhood, a secret organization that works against Big Brother. O'Brien proposes a toast: "What shall it be this time? To the confusion of the Thought Police? To the death of Big Brother? To humanity? To the future?" O'Brien essentially asks to toast to everything that the Brotherhood stands for: the confusion of the Thought Police and the death of Big Brother are the organization's goals, and it fights for humanity and the future. But Winston proposes a whole new toast entirely: to the past. O'Brien then says something completely radical: "the past is more important."

No matter how many times I read other books or fill my head with new words, those words always stick. "The past is more important." Winston declines to toast to everything the Brotherhood stands for, everything that Winston himself previously stood for, and instead proposes something more important: the past. Winston's entire life up to this point has been in spite of Big Brother; he wants to work against Big Brother, even if he is a minority of one. Despite all that the Brotherhood stands for, despite everything he has worked towards, Winston wants to toast to the past.

O'Brien saying that the past is more important than everything they have been fighting for and against has so many meanings. The goal of the Party is to continually change the past to maintain their power. They convince the population that the past didn't happen, and thus they claim the future as their own. But Winston works for the Party and knows how they change the past. Winston himself goes back, sometimes years, into newspapers and rewrites history. He knows, even if he won't admit it out loud, that the Party and everything it stands for has been fabricated. That's what makes him so important — he knows that the past the Party has shown to the public is not real, and that the Party can never truly change the past.

That's what makes the past so important. That's what makes the past more important than humanity or the future — no matter how much people try to change history, history does not change for people. People exist as a result of history, yet history exists on its own.

Keep Your Bearings

ROBERT NORSWORTHY

In the sheer range of possible approaches for telling a story, choosing one is often a sticking point for me. In such situations, I like to use a narrative technique, basic story feature, or piece of writing advice as a conceptual landmark for the way forward. It's easier for me to begin when there is something I plan to include. For example, I'll think to myself, "It's kind of neat when someone in an argument suddenly agrees with the other person, and you instantly see the whole interaction in a different light. I'd like to give that a try." Whether I'm setting a fictional critter loose in the suburbs or determining the pivotal moment of a duchess storming a roller rink, I can reassure myself that, if nothing else, I'll get to try my take on the specific feature I wish to incorporate.

When I am planning or analyzing a story, one concept I often think about comes from a Sam Smiley quotation: "The quickest and best way to know someone is to see that person make a significant decision." Does a character run a red light or arrive late? Does a character volunteer to investigate the sobbing in the cave or draw straws to see who goes? In these select moments, the suspense of wondering what a character will do leads to insight about how that character might act later.

When I consider this concept, my mind often returns to a certain moment from Terry Pratchett's *Carpe Jugulum*. The passage shows how striking a character's decision can be and how much, when executed masterfully, it can bring to the subject matter. The novel's antagonists are vampires led by the Count de Magpyr. In an example of Pratchett's typical analysis and parody of familiar subject matter, these vampires are determined to overcome their kind's failings. They condition themselves against the usual vampire weaknesses such as garlic and holy symbols, and they subjugate whole human communities into what they deem a peaceful alliance — one in which the humans obediently line up to act as the vampires' regular blood supply. These innovative, dangerous characters have made interesting choices, but I would like to discuss a pivotal decision of the character who opposes them.

Esmerelda Weatherwax, also known as Granny Weatherwax or simply Granny, is a witch, and a recurring character in the Discworld novels. Pratchett's witches take on many roles in their respective communities. These roles include opposing supernatural threats, healing, dealing with criminals, and comforting those close to death. As an accomplished witch, Granny has faced many grim situations, and *Carpe Jugulum* discusses how much she defines herself by the choices she has made in those situations. In the Discworld, she is wary of becoming corrupt, going "to the bad," which involves things like cackling and living in gingerbread houses. For this novel, Pratchett establishes a basic metaphor for Granny's internal conflict: to painstakingly determine and choose the right course of action is to face a harsh light, and to succumb to unbridled corruption is to turn toward the darkness.

When Granny confronts the vampires, the Count and the other vampires attack her in order to make her a vampire under their control. As she lies unconscious after the attack, she finds herself literally standing between light and darkness, on the verge of death or of becoming a vampire, with Death the character speaking to her. The darkness represents the inner aspects of herself that she has kept at bay, and the overwhelmingly brilliant light, she feels, may be the light that represents the way to leave life and all its torments behind. Death instructs her to choose, so she makes the latest in a lifetime of difficult decisions: she faces the light while stepping back into the dark.

There are a few reasons that this moment has stuck with me. For one thing, in terms of decisions defining a character, this is a rather literal example. It demonstrates that Granny Weatherwax is someone who chooses to confront the depths of corruption, including those within herself, while always trying to keep track of the way back from it — but not to the point that she fully enters the light and leaves her life, and all the conflicts that come with it, behind. By stepping backward into the dark, she faces the unsavoury thoughts that indicate her potential for corruption and recognizes that those thoughts are the same that have plagued her for a lifetime. In doing so, she identifies the nefarious voice in her head as herself and declares that she is no longer afraid of that person.

The vampires nearly turn Granny into a vampire under their control, but, through her chosen course of action, Granny proves capable of weathering that sinister power. She confronts the part of her that is drawn to it without allowing that aspect of herself to overpower her. Afterward, she pushes toward a different indicator of the light of life that she hopes to resume. Throughout, she maintains her sense of black-and-white thinking and later states that what some people call grays are simply a dirty form of white. Then, through this choice (I don't want to give too much of the story away), her character can shine in extraordinary ways that add an interesting development to Pratchett's vampires.

I admire how much this decision accomplishes as a turning point in Granny's battle against the Count and his clan. In one of my writing classes, I recall going over one of my fight scenes. I had striven to introduce the key ideas and to polish the scene's sound, pacing, clarity of description, tone, etc. Then my professor told me that she would typically skim over these kinds of scenes, as much of their content was usually superfluous to the main plot. I often appreciate action scenes in and of themselves, so the idea of skimming over an action scene shocked me. Naturally, I hope to avoid such a reader reaction, so I keep that feedback in mind when I consider which action scene approaches are most engaging and efficient. If I find myself mapping out a whole saloon and plotting the individual trajectories of several mercenary acrobats, I know that my efforts may be more fruitful if I ensure that any details about a spin kick or uppercut include new, key information that readers will want to keep in mind. Otherwise, I might be able to dodge the trouble of writing the fight scene at all — or at least including so much detail.

When I'm navigating the mire of myriad storytelling possibilities, it's discouraging to think that a section isn't worth the effort of writing it. The whole time I'm deliberating over whether to change perspectives, cover all the information through dialogue, summarize the whole scene, et cetera, I also know that I may end up cutting the part altogether. Having a single key purpose, such as defining a character through that character's decisions and ensuring that everything works in the service of that feature, gives me more confidence as I decide where to focus my efforts.

This moment from *Carpe Jugulum* provides an excellent example of this idea. The scene boils down to Granny standing on black sand, between bright light and shadow. Death personified stands alongside her and shows her an image of her body lying where she left it. Pratchett often depicts intricate realms and dynamic fight scenes, but here, Granny's choice is pivotal, so he focuses on that. The atypical way he portrays these vampires warrants an atypical form of decisive action in resisting them. Granny's decision is necessary, because the vampires are determined not to have a typical vampire confrontation: they lack the typical vampire weaknesses and can easily overpower physical assaults. The Count has even fortified his mind against Granny's powerful, direct mental attacks. The pivotal moment of Granny's opposition is the decision that allows her to confront and overcome the vampires' attempt to corrupt her, so this moment is placed in the foreground.

This decision has also remained with me because it breaks implied rules. It presents a situation as binary: a character stands on the border between two extremes and must make a choice. However, Pratchett has Granny Weatherwax actually stand at that point, and this decision allows for a literal, practical interpretation of the situation: if one is standing and able to walk in either direction, one is logically able to walk backward. I find it helpful to see Pratchett confront Granny's darkness by exploring options besides marching his character into the worst-case scenario. His choice works in this situation by giving a unique insight into Granny and into the novel's themes of choice, power, responsibility, and corruption. This moment exemplifies the outside-the-box thinking to be expected from Granny Weatherwax and from Pratchett.

Maybe it seems odd to spend so much time discussing a single piece of writing advice, but it's easy to feel bogged down by what should be done to get a plot where it needs to be. I'll find myself thinking, "the visiting warrior has to join the march against town hall because I need her to see the fleeing councilman meet up with a shadowy figure who has ties to an area-wide conspiracy," and so on. I need to remind myself that unless I think about what drives the protagonist, exactly why a visiting bystander would want to risk criminal charges by butting into a local uprising she's barely heard about, there's a good chance I'll cease to see the point in writing any of it. Granny Weatherwax's forward-focused, backward stride is a reminder of how much a well-written character can accomplish. Such strong examples of executing storytelling concepts help me make my own writing choices. With the countless shrouded paths that a story could follow, keeping my sights on one overarching objective helps me choose which steps to take.

Sense and Scents of Place

STEPHANIE OLIVER

My parents took me home from the Serendipity Memorial Hospital to a house full of secrets. I was a reeking bundle, which gave them something to talk about, something on which to focus their discontent and give it a voice. My sour body stank up the whole house. The unpleasant cat pee odour oozed from my pores and flowed into every room. It coiled around the loveseat where my mother liked to curl on rainy afternoons rescrolling through her favourite murder mysteries and penny romances. It gushed into the kitchen and ran over the counters. It sneaked through the narrowest cracks into all the cupboards, leached through airtight lids into cookie jars and flour canisters, rice buckets and spice bottles. It crept under the bedroom doors into the private rooms of each family member. It rushed up their nostrils and in through their ears. It poured down their throats when they opened their mouths to speak.

(*Salt Fish Girl* by Larissa Lai)

If I tell you I'm a Newfoundlander, something might smell fishy. Thanks to careful planning by my parents — Cape Bretoners who moved to Newfoundland to teach in the 1970s — my sisters and I were born in Nova Scotia and raised on the Rock. So, even though they brought me back to Newfoundland at a month old, technically I'm a Come From Away. Yet, Newfoundland has always been home.

I have lived away from Newfoundland for over two decades now, but whenever I step off the plane at Deer Lake airport, I'm immediately aware that I'm home, and it's my nose that tells me so. The tarmac is surrounded by dark green walls of boreal forest, blue-grey mountains rising in the distance. The ocean is nowhere in sight. But the smell — that fresh, crisp, salty sea air — lets me know I'm finally home.

When I was growing up on Bay St. George, the smell of the ocean was just a piece of the sensory puzzle, one of many unremarkable characteristics of my island home. The scent of salty sea air blended, unnoticed, into the background of my life. I'd stumble out of bed, blind to the perennial sunshine. I'd hurtle downstairs, ignoring the mountains in the window. I'd wolf down breakfast, oblivious to the waves peeking through the trees. I'd trip out the door, brushing off the salty breeze. My home was mere metres from the ocean, and I took it for granted.

I was much more aware of scents in transition. My memory became a storehouse of smells marked by summer visits to Cape Breton. The odd, vacant scent of our house when the alarm clock blared, rousing us for the early drive to the ferry. The overwhelming odour of gasoline and the fishy smell of rust rushing into the car when Dad rolled down the window, boarding instructions barked over deafening industrial engines. The assault of exhaust as we escaped the vehicle, threading through transport trucks to seek solace in the ship. Finally, a reprieve: the cabin interior. Stale air thick with armchair leather, cigarette smoke, snoring breath.

As we settled in, so did the smells. When Mom lifted the lid of the Coleman cooler, the scent of porous 1980s plastic (certainly not BPA free), stubbornly refusing to release the olfactory traces of past lunches, mixed with our meals: sour smell of darkening bananas, sweet-and-nutty aroma of peanut butter and jam sandwiches. Ziplock bags failed to protect the bread from this infusion of odours, so I tasted them too, all while the enticing aroma of fries and gravy from the cafeteria teased me. Once the ship set sail, we were free to roam. When I was a child, the plastic scent of the ball pit marked my time in the playroom. When I was a teen, the metallic smell of quarters marked my hands in the arcade. I was surrounded by salty sea air, but I barely smelled it — though on the rare occasion we went out on deck, the whipping wind wouldn't let us forget.

The sensory journey continued when we arrived in Cape Breton. As we approached my father's village of Point Tupper, we were welcomed — or rather, accosted — by a sulphurous stench. The unrelenting odour of the pulp mill, a stinging trace of the industrialization that destroyed local economies when the causeway opened. My sisters and I were at the mercy of the stench on hot summer nights when we needed the breeze to sleep. Yet, the stink was also strangely comforting, as it accompanied plates of ribbon sandwiches delivered by my doting grandmother, bowls of ice cream scooped by my quiet grandfather, and buckets of blueberries gathered by throngs of cousins. The blueberry hills hid the mill that we never saw but always smelled. We'd become accustomed to the stench just in time to leave for my mother's home.

Tucked into a bucolic bay, her home in River Bourgeois was also just steps from industry, but on a much smaller scale. The working wharf down the road greeted us with a sweet and fishy bouquet of gasoline and rust that recalled the scent of the ferry but was more muted, more pleasant. Blending with the salty scent of seaweed and the fetid odour of shells left by the tide, the redolent breeze wafted into my grandmother's kitchen window, mixing with the buttery aroma of warm biscuits, the bright scent of fresh strawberries, and the irresistible fragrance of fried mackerel — a cherished olfactory recipe. These sensory journeys eventually ended, but my memory absorbed as much as our Coleman cooler. This olfactory archive remained buried until I discovered *Salt Fish Girl*, a novel that brought me home.

For most of my life, I steered clear of books about fish. I struggled to see how fishing — which seemed to be *the* defining characteristic of Newfoundland literature — was relevant to my life as a millennial teen. I didn't grow up in an outport, I didn't like cod, and the only iceberg I'd seen was in *Titanic*. I wanted to experience the world, and good grades were my ticket. I left to study English at university in Nova Scotia, where I avoided Canadian literature altogether and took every course I could on American literature. "America" represented a sexy cosmopolitanism that epitomized the opposite of my isolated youth. On my bookshelves, there was nary a fish to be found. Increasingly, I spent time in basement computer labs writing essays on sanitized screens, the air-conditioning masking all odours. When the sweet smell of manure perfumed the air each spring, I knew only a few finals stood between me and my future. I'd head home to my job as a summer camp counsellor, plotting plans while giving little thought to the salty sea air surrounding me.

After graduation, I moved to London, Ontario for graduate school. While my mind expanded, my sensory world shrank as I buried my nose in my books. The mass-produced paperbacks faded into the background of my life as quickly as the hot ink on my photocopies. All my time was spent in air-conditioned classrooms and computer labs; I lived on sanitized screens. As I moved from the MA into the PhD, I trained myself to, quite literally, focus — at the expense of my senses. I spent hours, months, weeks, years in front of a computer screen, shoulders hunching, spine curving, legs folding, fingers typing as I contorted my body into a life of the mind. I barely took breaks, let alone trips home. I was stuck.

This stuckness manifested in my PhD field study exam. I wanted to study gender and embodiment in American literature, but I struggled to find inspiring texts. And according to my committee, I needed to think more about "the body," a concept I had only theorized in abstract terms. I can recall the setting of the exam — orderly wooden book-shelves filled with hardcover tomes, long wooden table with rounded edges, hard wooden chair keeping me upright — but I can't recall a single smell. I do, however, remember the questions that hung in the air. "How might you think about embodiment in a more specific way?" "What about sensory experience?" I felt something open inside me. In all that I'd read about the body, what had been said about the senses?

I recalled a philosopher deemed radical for re-orienting studies of embodiment toward touch. When I cracked open his book the next day, memories of other readings came rushing back. There were countless studies of vision and hearing, and there was ample research on taste. But scholars barely mentioned smell. So, I followed my nose to the campus library, where I checked out the few books on scent.

They all gave similar reasons for smell's status as a footnote. *Highly subjective. Linked to memory, emotion, association. Primitive, animalistic. Evokes fear, pleasure, desire, disgust. Diffuse, pervasive, invisible. Transgressive, uncontainable. Difficult to capture, categorize, measure.*

When I read that literature is one of the few ways to record scent alongside the claim that few olfactory words exist in English, my interest piqued. Energized, I headed to my faculty building and ran into a friend, bubbling over with excitement about my new direction.

"You need to read *Salt Fish Girl!*"

I'd never heard of it, but the title felt strangely familiar.

I sat down with *Salt Fish Girl*, pencil in hand. When I came across "I was a reeking bundle," I began writing in the margins… and kept going and going. Odours permeated the pages about memory, migration, bodies, and belonging. I had never read a story where scent was more than a feature of mood or atmosphere. Or had I just failed to notice? In *Salt Fish Girl*, scents not only *had* character; they *were* characters, bursting with energy and demanding attention. The smells had me hooked.

I already felt nostalgic pangs when I saw Newfoundland's wind-swept shores in tourism ads and heard its distinctive diction on *Republic of Doyle*. But after *Salt Fish Girl*, I began thinking about this relationship in terms of smell. London's rare foggy days almost tricked me into smelling salt in the air, Lake Erie's sea-like size deceived my eyes but never my nose, and Highway 7's sweet grasses and grains were unlike the olfactory nature of Newfoundland coastline.

The smells of *Salt Fish Girl* prompted me to think more about diasporas, communities that feel both connected to and displaced from their homelands. The longer I lived away, the more I felt part of something that resembled a diasporic community. Thanks to the geographic isolation I once resented, Newfoundlanders are known for their unique linguistic and cultural identity, strong sense of community, and deep connection to the Rock — a connection that only seems to intensify when they leave. And, as Lai's novel reminds readers, legacies of imperialism and colonialism enable people like me — a descendant of mostly Scottish, French, and British settlers — to feel at home there in the first place.

As I marked olfactory passages, my pencil paused on another strangely familiar kind of reference: Ville d'Espoir, an island that changes hands between the French and English numerous times, to the point that the name (ironically) signifies "hope" in its French spelling and "despair" in its English pronunciation. Was this a reference to Bay D'Espoir, the Newfoundland settlement with a similar story? Something smelled fishy. I immediately searched Lai online and couldn't believe what I read: "Born in La Jolla, California, raised in St. John's, Newfoundland." The book led me home.

A One-Point Perspective

GILLIAN BURROWS

I used to like to draw his picture when he was in a dangerous mood, for then I could get his personality down in a few lines.

(*The Outsiders* by S.E. Hinton)

*T*he *Outsiders* is one of those books you need to read twice in order to feel the full impact. The circular narrative and formatting — an autobiographical essay submission — add a layer of depth to the text that is easily underestimated, and I'm certain that if my seventh-grade class hadn't been shown the movie (the script is essentially a second edition of the novel, revised by Hinton in adulthood) within hours of finishing the novel, the influence of the story would have been lost on me as soon as the unit was over.

Rather than a simple recollection of events, *The Outsiders* serves as a real-time analysis of the past as it coincides with the present. The protagonist, Ponyboy (yes, that is his real name), exists in two places at once: the present, as he narrates the story, and the past, as he lives within it. Despite only a few weeks passing between the time the story starts and when Ponyboy records it, there is a clear separation between the Ponyboy in the story and the Ponyboy who tells it. Forced to grow up and understand the world anew, Ponyboy experiences a rapid-fire coming of age after witnessing the sudden — and unnecessary — deaths of three people, one his closest friend.

The premise of the story, therefore, is that it isn't just a story. It's a method of preservation, one focused on facts and truth rather than a romanticized ideal. Ponyboy aims to tell the story as objectively as he can, partially out of necessity — the assignment is a way for him to redeem himself both academically and socially — and partially because he wants to remember the people he lost as they were, not as he wanted them to be or as a stranger might see them. Ponyboy wants to show the people he lost not as fictionalized versions of themselves but as real people with real lives and real problems. Ponyboy's story is full of conflicting emotions and ideas, with the characters actively portrayed as many things at once, some contradictory: heroes are also hoodlums; villains are also victims. Characters are constantly evolving — just like people in real life.

This treatment of the characters is what struck me about Hinton's novel. After years of reading stories where good and bad were distinguished through a high-contrast lens, here was a story where those lines are endlessly blurred. The characters are fluid and multidimensional, a stark contrast to the bulky archetypes found in most novels meant for young adults. Interestingly, this same observation is partially what inspired Hinton to write *The Outsiders*. She wanted literature that captures the real and raw experience of adolescence and early adulthood: novels that show life as it is, not as the author thinks it should be.

I think to achieve this type of realism, there needs to be a separation between the author and the narrative. I'm not saying the author shouldn't be passionate about the story — the most compelling novels are always the ones you know the author had fun writing — but the author should step back and let the narrator have full control over the story. Hinton's involvement as an author in *The Outsiders* (and all her young adult novels, if I'm honest) is subtle. Her role in the narrative isn't to tell it, but rather to transcribe it: to bridge the gap between her characters' world and our own. In every aspect, the story belongs to the narrator. The author just provides an outlet.

In my writing, I try to do the same thing: tell the story from the one-point perspective of the narrator and focus on their individual experience. I've always preferred first-person point of view stories — both in reading and writing. I find they're much more intimate than the shadowy lens of a third-person narrator. With first-person, the story almost feels like a secret. The specific details become hidden knowledge that I, someone unrelated to the story, just happened to stumble upon. I like the innate trust that comes from the narrator telling me what should be considered private information. Character-driven stories told by someone directly involved with a "this is exactly how I swear it happened" bluntness: that's what I like.

I get asked all the time how I write such realistic characters, and there's an air of disbelief when I confess that I don't use character-building worksheets. I understand the purpose of them and how they can be helpful, but personally, I've found they hinder my creative process rather than help it. Putting together analytical, fact-based profiles confines the characters to the page and reduces their existence to their role in a story. I prefer to think of characters as real people with complex, multidimensional lives that exist beyond the timeframe of the narrative. The story has a start and an end, but there's also a before and after; an extended story that readers — and writers — will never get to see in the same intimate detail. The characters were different versions of themselves before the story started, and they will become different versions of themselves after the story ends. Their pasts and their futures are incomprehensible to anyone outside of their world but nonetheless still exist. The details on a planning page suggest permanence. They place a character inside a box with no escape.

I also find the overly specific nature of the questions on those worksheets has the potential to take away the narrator's credibility. How many of those details would the narrator actually know about the people around them? How many of those details could I fill in about people I know in real life? Probably not many, regardless of how close the relationship. In stories told from the perspective of a single character, the audience should only know as much as the narrator knows, and it's difficult to achieve that sense when you, the author, have made yourself into an all-knowing figure.

My method of writing realistic characters comes down to "Draft

Zero": a document where the story unfolds in fragments later pieced into a coherent narrative. In this draft, I find my characters and narrator through their involvement in the story and the way they interact with each other, as well as with the world around them. With the narrator specifically, I get to know them through their storytelling methods. Linguistic choices, the details they choose to focus on, the way they portray people and situations…these quirks help me understand my narrator in a way traditional character planning worksheets never will.

With non-narrator characters, I get to meet them from the narrator's perspective and therefore see the versions of themselves they choose to show to the people around them. I'm able to perceive these characters from the point of view of someone who interacts with them regularly and then conveys that information to an audience. I view them as a friend, a relative, an acquaintance. Their relationship to the narrator is their relationship to me.

Methods that allow flexibility and can easily be altered as I better understand the story help when it comes to keeping track of characters — playlists full of songs that describe the character and their personal music taste; vision boards full of images of things they like; clothes they would wear; quotations they might relate to. I look at the characters and piece them together the way a friend would, not as biographical facts, not as their deepest fears or hidden secrets. Instead, I focus on how Hinton's narrator would see them: as real people rather than fiction.

VI – HEALING

Remembering
CATHERINE COURTEAU

My clearest memories of Madi are captured by photographs. Perhaps I was too young at six years old to form detailed recollections. I have only two pictures of her. In the first, she's in a wheelchair on our dock. She's wearing a purple bathing cap to cover her bald head and a bathing suit with purple and yellow flowers. Much smaller than her chair, she's looking straight at the camera with a bright smile, as if caught laughing. I don't think people faked laughter for photographs more than twenty years ago. Anyway, her laugh in this picture is full of teeth and gums, real and spontaneous. There is no sadness in her eyes, in her pale face, no discouragement in the way she pulls back her concave shoulders. Years later, my parents told me this photograph was taken during her last summer. Her cancer had relapsed, and her family had chosen to spend that summer at the lake together rather than in and out of hospitals. She loved that lake — its emerald sparkles at first light and its indigo shades after sunset. On warm days, she'd spend hours digging her feet in the chilly layers of slippery mud underwater. And there she was, sitting in front of her lake, with her gigantic smile and her flip flops flipping an inch from the ground.

The second photograph, of poor quality, shows Madi, her sister and me playing in the lake. The movement of water and bodies makes the image blurry with fun. We swim around Madi, whose floaters, tightly wrapped around her small arms, barely keep her above water. I don't remember feeling sadness when she was still alive, nor pity, nor anger. At that age, I couldn't grasp the gravity of illness, the finitude of death. It didn't bother me that she had tubes feeding her oxygen, as long as we searched for dock spiders Sunday afternoons. As long as we could play, everything would be okay.

My father tells me that at her funeral I ran to her coffin and let out a scream that broke his heart. When I saw her immobile little body, the entire trajectory of her long illness flashed before me. Nothing made sense — Madi's sister, her parents, and my own family had exchanged their bathing suits for formal black clothes. I banged and banged on the minuscule coffin until my father carried me, a limp bag of tears and snot, back to the pew.

Living away from home, I'm often subject to a nostalgic pull towards my childhood memorabilia. Last Thanksgiving, I visited my parents at their cottage on Sunday afternoon; my mother was outside cutting down spent flower heads and stalks. My father was piling up firewood in neat rows by the basement door. I went up to my childhood room, where I browsed through my high school portfolio: essays on *The Lady of the Camellias, The Life Before Us, The Death of Ivan Ilyich*. A common thread in my selection of books was a deep curiosity about stories concerning the end of life. I wondered if this preference was because I had not been present for the end of Madi's. I reached for my copy of *The Life Before Us*. A passage was highlighted in yellow that tells of how fourteen-year-old Momo thinks that the dying Madame Rosa does not look good, how Momo lights candles for company and applies make-up to her adoptive mother's face, making the eyelids blue and white, how she glues tiny stars on the eyelids and attempts to add false eyelashes, including after Madame Rosa has stopped breathing. Momo continues to love her even after the breath stops, and so lies down beside the body with an umbrella she calls Arthur. Then, Momo tries to feel even worse than she does so that she can be completely dead. She lights more and more candles as they continue to be snuffed.

Some people might feel fear, disgust, or incomprehension reading a somewhat morbid passage. I was overwhelmed with envy. Momo, at the young age of fourteen, was able to care for her dying adoptive mother. I couldn't help wondering why I had not been able to care for Madi. Why hadn't I been allowed to colour her eyelids in blue and white, draw waves on her bony cheeks and glue stickers on her nails? Why hadn't I been able to say goodbye?

The moments between that sunny August at the cottage and Madi's funeral seem to have slipped from my memory. Now that I am a palliative care physician, I have many questions: Did Madi die at home? In hospice? In the intensive care unit? Suddenly? Unexpectedly? From a progressive decline? Did she suffer? Did she die alone? Was she surrounded by family? Twenty-three years after her death, I possess no answers. All I have are two pictures and the memories woven in between.

Never did I manage to ask Madi's family for more photographs. In fact, I have not talked to her family about her since that time. I learned that there are words too painful to speak: in the years after she passed, no one dared say her name. As I progressed from childhood to adulthood, the right moment to mention her seemed perpetually out of reach. Some tragedies must be left buried, undisturbed.

According to Buddhist Jack Kornfield, in the Jewish mystical tradition, one great Rabbi taught his disciples to memorize and contemplate his teachings and place prayers and holy words on their hearts. One day, a student asked the Rabbi why he used the phrase "on your heart" rather than "in your heart." The master replied, "Only time and grace can put the essence of these stories in your heart. Here, we recite and learn them and put them on our hearts, hoping that someday, when our heart breaks, they will fall in."

One can only process life events with the physical and emotional capacity one has at any given moment. Derived from loss or from literature, meaning seeps into our hearts gradually, as they become open and receptive. I continue reading Romain Gary: Momo kisses Madame Rosa, but it doesn't help. The face is cold, yet the woman's kimono and red wig are beautiful. Momo sleeps on the mattress beside the corpse, and every time he wakes up, he adds more and more make-up, to rectify the increasing grey-bluish tint. She's afraid to go out, because there's no one there. I felt Momo's solitude deeply,

THE ALCHEMY OF STORIES

the loneliness of being the one left behind. Surely, I would have found Madi beautiful too. I hope she wore something colourful.

For decades after her death, I could not form a conscious thought of Madi. There would be the odd moment in school when the word "cancer" would pop up and provoke a spiral of uncontrollable sobbing; once, my mother had to take me home for the rest of the day. Through the car window, I watched pedestrians go about their normal affairs. I would not speak her name.

In medical school, I was intuitively drawn to palliative care, just as I had been pulled towards all those end-of-life books in high school. I wanted to support patients and their families at the end, but I could not explain why. In an act of belated redemption or an attempt to ease an open wound, I transformed my grief into a sacred dedication to the care of the dying. I became acutely aware of the immense privilege it is to be present for someone's last, precious moments. More than twenty years after Madi left us, I officially started grief therapy and embarked on my palliative care training. With each therapy session, her name became a little easier to speak. I no longer choked on the word. Memories resurfaced.

In *The Life Before Us*, Madame Rosa reassures her adopted daughter Momo that it's not necessary to have reasons to be afraid. When I felt too raw to face my grief, literature allowed me to approach the topic at my own pace. My gentle and gradual exploration of death and dying through literature allowed me to remember. It led me back to Madi.

The Pinners

MARISA BORDONARO

I am walking to the elevators with The Pinners now, in a few more minutes I will be the butterfly, wing tip to wing tip pinned on the giant board. They will look and find nothing, the famous Dr. Carter will shake his head in confusion. I feel no shiver in the pit of my stomach as I have on other Pinning Days — this will be my fourth time on the giant board. Yes, I am getting used to it.

(*The Butterfly Ward* by Margaret Gibson)

We sat in a line of ash-coloured cots, with plastic shields between us. Cracks on the ceiling branched out like spiderwebs. Every so often, a figure in the dark would stumble to the bathroom, tailed by a sharp-eyed nurse. Other nurses chattered at the desk. At one point, they burst out laughing. I kept an eye on the camera pointed at me, my limp body against a sea of gray blankets in the frame, trying to discern the object of their laughter.

I first encountered the Pinners two summers ago. After a childhood characterized by counting out four brisk knocks on doors for good luck and squeezing my eyes shut against six o'clock and six-sided die to avoid Hell, an adolescence defined by recoiling from the shapeless body I saw in the mirror, and a young adulthood shaped by all of the above, I found myself dropped off at the psychiatric section of the hospital and assigned a bed.

In the morning, I was allowed to call my parents. I walked up to the nurse guarding the phone for the patients.

"Can I use the phone?" I said meekly. I hated my reed-thin voice, the way my body shrunk from the five-foot-two woman, the grimace that made her appear a foot taller to me.

"What?" she said loudly. "Do I see the phone? We've lost it?" She scanned the desk with its scattered papers, capless pens, and steel water bottle.

The phone — a clunky, outdated model — lay adjacent to the water bottle. With flushed cheeks and a strong desire to slink back to my bed, I watched her survey the room. As soon as I mustered the will to say, "No, I said can I *use* it, it's right there," she spotted it.

"It's right there. Can't you see it?" She shook her head and turned back to her papers.

I managed a strained smile. "Oh, yeah, sorry. Thanks." As I grabbed it, I choked out another "really sorry!"

For the next few hours, whenever I had to interact with her, I peppered my responses with "sorry": "I'm sorry to bother you, but can I use the phone again? No worries if it's already being used!" "Hello, sorry, but could I get a glass of water? Thanks so much, and sorry again!"

The apologies must have softened her, because when it was my time to leave, she smiled at me and chatted about what a nice day it was outside, about how the heat had finally died down. I nodded and smiled, but I kept remembering the newest patient who, an hour prior, had wandered around the room, zigzagging between chairs, wires, and people, stopping to ask nurse after nurse if she could be moved from a cot to one of the few beds that were available. Each nurse had chirped the same familiar response, "We'll tell you when we can move you, dear!" The patient had stared silently in response before continuing her journey.

Except this nurse. Facing the woman's five-second stare, the nurse barked, "We are not having a staring contest! Get back to bed."

A quiet patient is a good patient, I thought, as the nurse and I walked through the front doors of the hospital. We passed a row of purple and red flowers, drenched in sunlight. A few moths flitted back and forth.

A few months ago, leading up to my primary field exam in Canadian literature for my PhD, my apartment transformed into a fortress of books. A musty copy of John Richardson's *Wacousta* huddled under a pile of papers on the desk, scrawled with purple ink. At least thirty slim yellow sticky notes bedecked Charles Gordon's *Glengarry School Days*, positioned on top of the bookcase. Directly underneath, Milton Wilson's *Poets Between the Wars* stood half the height of the other books, its title crammed on the slim spine in almost-illegible print.

Most evenings, I sat up in my bed, knees glued to my chest, wrapping myself in a tinier and tinier ball.

"Does anyone even care about Canadian literature?" was a recurring theme in my phone conversations with my friend Kel. One evening in mid-February, my question changed to "do *I* even care about Canadian literature?" "What if everything I'm doing is meaningless?" I asked. My muscles grew tenser and tenser until it felt like my bones fused into my skin. "I can't make anyone care about anything. I'm useless."

Kel's voice softened. "Our brains can suck sometimes. If you don't want to continue the program, that's valid. But you're not useless." A sudden yowl in the background. "Ash! What are you doing?" After a pause, she returned. "Sorry, the cat tried to attack the cardboard box that he sleeps in."

I chuckled, even though I felt for the little guy. Earlier that day, I had attacked my bookshelf, arranging and rearranging the heaps in an attempt to slot in Margaret Laurence's *The Diviners*. The whole pile had toppled over, books scattering across the floor like rats.

"Maybe the goal isn't to finish the program," Kel said. "Maybe it's to find something to keep you moving forward."

Something pinched my palms, and I looked down to see my nails digging into my skin. Several half-crescents formed, like the upper halves of butterfly wings.

A few days later, surrounded by walls of books in the living room, I opened *The Butterfly Ward*, a collection of short stories published in 1976. Since my flimsy research topic was "depictions of mental illness in Canadian poetry," while preparing my exam reading list months prior, I had hunted for not only poems but novels, short stories, and autobiographies that alluded to mental illness. After hundreds of internet searches, my keyword variations grew more and more fragmented, deteriorating from "mental illness in Canadian literature," "Canadian fiction depression," "Canada + asylum + books," to "mad + Canada."

I stumbled upon Margaret Gibson.

A 2006 *Toronto Star* article, "Demons Drove Gifted Writer's Career," described Gibson's struggles with mental illness. She had been institutionalized at fifteen for paranoid schizophrenia and had navigated a lifetime of psychotic episodes. She possessed a desire to shape her pain into writing — a life-draining task, but one that would, in her own words, "make the blood sing."

Now, as I flipped through the book, butterflies flew across the pages and transformed the characters' unquantifiable aches and anxieties into wings that beat faster and faster until exploding into uncontrollable rage, flailing limbs pinned to a bed in the neurological ward where "The Pinners" prepare to prick the patient's brain with needles for scanning. The conquered patient lies still as a dead butterfly in a collector's box, succumbing to its own captivity.

The Pinners, faceless doctors hovering over patients, transformed onto the page when the nurse of my past materialized. *It's right there. Can't you see it?*

But my Pinners were never as aggressive, I thought. *Is it fair for me to try to create my own meaning from them when I ultimately escaped their grasp by keeping quiet and still?* I pondered the question. Finding a notebook that wasn't littered with chapter-by-chapter summaries of books or weekly to-do lists, I began to write.

At first, my sentences consisted of simple, plain phrases: "They wheeled me to a room. It was dark." I slammed my pen on the coffee table then flipped through *The Butterfly Ward* again. I could see Dr. Carter, beyond the pinning board of the 1976 text, inside the office of my new family physician, two years ago. When he entered the office, he smiled at my mother and me, as if the ivory white walls, delicate white paper on the examination bed, and white-framed painting of greenery were actually an orchid garden, crisp and inviting.

"Sorry for the long wait time. Glad you haven't run out. You wouldn't be the first to do so." He chuckled, and I felt my shoulders lighten. "You're just going to have to remind me why you're here."

"She has very low self-esteem," said my mother.

"*You* do, or her?"

I said, "I do. I mean, I guess I have anxiety and depression diagnoses."

He pulled up my files and my diagnoses on the computer. His fingernails clicked on the keyboard like talons.

"So, what do you do?" he asked.

"I guess I get stressed out a lot."

"No, I mean, do you work? Are you in school?"

"Yeah, I'm moving to London for my PhD in a few months."

"A *P-H-D*?" The clicking ceased between each of the letters. "In what?"

"English."

"Wow. What do you have to be depressed about?" He smiled and shook his head. "A PhD is such an accomplishment."

I waited for "that's what I would say if I was one of those supervillain doctors who doesn't have access to the Internet and says depressed people 'just need to get over it.'"

"Some people I see, they're on welfare, they're failing out of school, they've blown up their own lives. But you, you're going somewhere."

Directly across from me, next to signs for breast cancer screenings and osteoporosis, a big blue sign plastered across the wall read, "Recognize the Symptoms of Mental Illness." The whiteness that enveloped the room grew brighter and brighter until all that remained was the stock image of a sad face directly in the center of the sign. I remembered the young woman's stony face in the psychiatric ward, the thin smiles of the nurses, the sharp "we are not having a staring contest!"

"That doesn't matter," I said. "I'm not better than anyone else."

I wanted to write something that displayed the smallness of the

Dr. Carters in their smudged coats, uncombed hair, and unmatched socks as they sat at their computers and constructed their notions of madness. Good patients and bad patients. So-called "real" patients and "accomplished" ones. But I hadn't really responded to the doctor at all. I only wished I had.

Yet, putting words on the page released me from my silence.

My Pinners may not have physically constrained me or paralyzed me with angry words, but they still pinned me. My own words, and the words of other writers, liberated our experiences from medical diagnoses and lists of symptoms. My formerly flimsy research topic — depictions of mental illness in Canadian poetry — seemed to gain substance. Did Margaret Gibson imagine The Pinners in coming decades as shape-shifters, shuffling some patients into categories and others into the silence of their beds? Did she imagine her written words shouting back at them?

Her words ignited me. They *made the blood sing*.

The Last Strait of Loneliness

LACEY FROST

Hypochondria has that wont, to rise in the midst of thousands — dark as Doom, pale as Malady, and well nigh strong as Death. Her comrade and victim thinks to be happy one moment — "Not so," says she; "I come." And she freezes the blood in his heart and beclouds the light in his eye.

(*Villette* by Charlotte Brontë)

For most of my life, I have struggled with depression. At least, that is my explanation when I wish to be plainly understood. But if I had time and someone to listen, I would rather tell them that, when I was a child, frustrated and confused by the invisible rules that governed the social world, I suspected that everyone had received a guidebook to life, and mine had been lost in the mail. If my listener would hear more, I would share my later fantasy that I was an alien experimentally sent to Earth, only to remain until my home planet recalled me. I would confess that, well into my teenage years, I ended the hardest days by looking to the sky and begging my extraterrestrial family to take me home.

I do not feel as though my melancholy follows me unbidden. What I term "depression" is the mess of loneliness, homesickness and exhaustion natural to one struggling in a strange world. As I entered adolescence, my feelings of isolation became unbearable, and I resolved to fit in by any means. Merciless in my efforts to make myself lovable, I lied to people, I starved myself, I strove to imitate the people around me, always clinging to the desperate belief that if I looked and spoke and acted like everyone else, I would be accepted.

But I was wrong. Connection to others — deep connection for which I yearned — proved unreachable. It was as though a thick pane of dirty glass separated me from the rest of the world: I might observe, imitate, even attract passing notice, but no matter how I banged and clamoured, I could touch nothing. As my physical and mental health deteriorated, I came to believe that Fate had destined me to misery.

By my sixteenth birthday, I acknowledged my exile as a life sentence, and I longed to end my suffering. After years of ineffectual therapy, I was referred to a mental health crisis team. Blindly trusting that these people would fix me, I trudged through the months-long waiting list.

How can I describe the weight of my disappointment when, after nearly succumbing to despair and barely maintaining my hold on a singular lifeline, I saw this last hope dashed before my eyes by the only people I thought could help me? The psychiatric team offered nothing but swift diagnoses and generic advice. When I finally shared the feelings I had hidden for so long, they informed me that I was mistaken: people with my diagnoses did not think as I claimed.

Sobs broke from me as I gripped the arms of my plastic chair, one of a circle that otherwise held professionally condescending women, each offering a pitying smile. They had no idea how I hated them. Crueler than the rest of the world, which merely shunned me for failing to fit in, they demanded that I do so and refused to believe I couldn't. I realized then that I would never be understood.

One benefit arose from my acknowledgment that acceptance was unattainable: I could give up the unhealthy means I had employed to seek it. I settled on a compromise. I would cease my belligerent grasping for connection but hide the parts of myself that would exacerbate my alienation. I buried my feelings of anguish, too ugly for others to bear, and forced myself to smile.

I never lost sight of the darkness that plagued me, but, slowly, my fixation waned. My mind's voices grew soft and indistinct. Each time I buried them, they took longer to resurrect. Finally, I forced my darkest thoughts into a corner of my mind, drew bars against them, and refused them all but the smallest and most rare acknowledgement. For the next five years, I maintained a careful balance between indulgence and suppression of my prisoners as I struggled for resignation.

Then, around my twenty-second birthday, I read *Villette*, and everything came crashing down. Lucy Snowe — the narrator whose melancholy rivals my own — gripped my attention and held it fast as she forced me to recall every thought and feeling I had suppressed. As I faced plain, stoical and honest Lucy, she spoke their names: "shrinking sloth and cowardly insolence," a haunting dread of one's "outward deficiency," "a sorrowful indifference to existence," a "soon-depressed, easily deranged temperament." These sentiments swiftly gained strength and broke free from their prison to race to the forefront of my mind.

I did not face them alone. Lucy clasped my hand as she told her story, and I seemed to behold in her my own reflection, sharing her "importunate gratitude" to anyone who pays a small kindness. Her fast attachment, her vain hope for reciprocity, and her struggle to suppress her feelings were familiar to me. After years of believing these trials unique to me, I met this discovery of kinship with tremendous relief.

In every step of Lucy's relationship with Dr. John, I recognized my cherished friendship with a roommate in the first year of university, and recalled the day I moved into residence, all nerves and excitement to find in our shared washroom a note that expressed her eagerness to meet me. I instantly knew we would be great friends.

And we were. We instantly clicked, and enjoyed discussing our families, favourite literature, and ambitions. Awfully grateful for her support throughout my first year, I allowed myself to enjoy her company mindlessly, to forget the deficiencies of my character I had thought intolerable, and to believe that she saw something in me that made the rest worth accepting.

But, as the year wore on, I gradually saw less of her. New friends — ones who possessed cheerful temperaments and social ease — began to occupy her time. She did not abruptly halt our interactions as Dr. John does with Lucy; our friendship died slowly, with absences, excuses, and interactions that gradually grew colder. Still, I trusted her reassurances and refused to believe that the friend I loved as a sister no longer cared for me, until the evidence became undeniable. Summer came, and we never spoke again.

Long did I scour my memory in a vain attempt to determine how I lost her. Finally, Lucy Snowe persuaded me to abandon my "imbecile extravagances of self-accusation." As I read her understanding of Dr. John, I realized that my friend had not bestowed her kindness out of partiality to me. Friendliness was in her nature, and I had been a convenient recipient. Like Dr. John, my friend belonged to the bright world I could never enter. Of course, she preferred to befriend people who could accompany her on her journey through it. It was unreasonable to expect that she might halt her progress to dwell with an exile. Like the shift of Dr. John's focus from Lucy to Paulina Mary, my friend's change was "right, just, natural; not a word could be said." But, just as Lucy continues her "incessant perusal" of Dr. John's letters long after they have ceased to arrive, I keep my roommate's note from the day we met, and still I smile to remember the time when I believed myself loved.

My supplications to Reason to prevent me from re-committing the same error have proven little more effective than Lucy's. The cycle of forming a hasty and intense attachment, struggling to suppress my feelings, and being left to despair when my acquaintance inevitably tires of me is constant and exhausting, and I confess, has led to bitterness. The advice I have received on the matter is little more helpful than Dr. John's encouragement to "cultivate happiness." But my kinship to Lucy allows me to receive from her lessons that I would refuse from any other.

She forced me to confront the resentment I had carried since that grudging acceptance of my fate. Lucy too must live as an outsider, knowing no more of life's happiness than what she can glean from distant observation, and yet she does not succumb to envy. Paulina Mary possesses everything Lucy wants: a loving home, beauty, and wealth, and Lucy must watch Paulina capture Dr. John's love as well. But, far from resenting Paulina, Lucy remains a good friend to her, and even helps convince her father to accept Dr. John as his son-in-law.

Once the engagement is confirmed, Lucy fades into the background to resume her place as an outsider.

Upon reading this scene, I was obliged to recognize my mishandling of parallel situations. Often I failed to remain a good friend to people more fortunate than me, or allowed a single display of affection to provoke me to jealous misery. Rather than assume my rightful place as observer and assistant, I have fled the scene to lament my solitude.

Soon after I finished *Villette*, in the restaurant where I work I happened to serve a young couple, whose near-perfect beauty, cheerful banter, and easy manners seemed particularly calculated to vex me. The woman appeared the embodiment of everything I have longed to be: beautiful, with long blonde hair tied in ribbons, and blue eyes that sparkled as she laughed, fashionably dressed, and in possession of a social ease that encouraged her companion's expressions of admiration. Her genuine smile and politeness made plain her affinity to the virtuous Paulina Mary: she both deserved love and possessed every attribute to keep it.

They were inclined to engage me in conversation, and I kept its focus on them. With every word of their discussion, which pertained to amorous topics I could not understand, I lost focus on their world and saw more clearly the dirty glass that kept me from it. The same thought I've conceived countless times struck me with particular force: *I would never be like them.*

When I inquired about their plans for the evening and they answered by naming, in unison, my favourite movie, the fourth wall broke — whatever higher power had sent them to torment me demanded my acknowledgement. I turned from the glass that displayed reality and searched the surrounding darkness. In the abyss, I beheld one figure — that of the small, plain Lucy Snowe, who had watched this interaction with detached stoicism. Upon catching my gaze, she sternly directed it back to reality.

As I resumed making polite inquiries and laughing at their banter, I felt Lucy's steady hand on my shoulder, and I knew that she approved of my effort to rally. I leaned on her support as we observed the scene before us; I "sealed my eyes and my ears, while I withdrew thence my thoughts, my sense of harmony still acknowledged in it a charm." When their giggling argument over the bill ensued, I was content to fade into the background, because my world of darkness and isolation held another resident.

Lucy Snowe is always with me. She names my errors when I cannot do so myself. She encourages me to accept my place with humility, to resist the bitterness of envy, and to support others' happiness, regardless of whether I might achieve the same. If I never find true companionship, I have her.

For the first time in years, I find it possible to express the feelings Lucy gave me words to describe. The prospect of rejection no longer terrifies me when I know that Lucy Snowe feels as I do. The reviews of *Villette* that criticize Lucy as irrational and snobbish only influence me to cling more tightly to her as one misunderstood in this world as well as her own. The reviewers do not comprehend her strength, her strategies for survival, and her prevailing virtue, but I understand her. I imagine she understands me. At the least, she helped me to better understand myself, and for that, I feel less alone.

I Never Wanted to Be a Writer, But I'm Doing It Anyway

CARRIE KIESWETTER

P ercy Jackson never wanted to be a half-blood, and I never wanted to be a writer.

My sixth-grade classroom was muggy, and it smelt like glue. I'd always liked the room. Miss Foster was new and visibly excited to start her job, so the classroom was impeccably decorated. It was covered in colourful posters, and little paper chain links hung from the corkboards. We had just started the unit on Greek mythology. In light of the heat weighing down our un-air-conditioned classroom, Miss Foster decided to give us a break and do some reading aloud. At first, my legs were stuck to my chair, because of the unfortunate combination of skin, plastic, and humidity. Then, they were stuck because I was utterly engrossed in the story. She was reading from *The Lightning Thief.* I'd never heard of Percy Jackson's novels, and it was the first time I recall feeling pulled in by a book — I mean that literally. I leaned forward, and it felt as though my vision narrowed. I'd always had "selective hearing," as my mom called it, but the only thing I could hear was the story. Even the puttering of the clunky fan in the corner faded into background noise. We'd talked about visualization in class before, but this time I *saw* the story playing in my head like a personal movie. I'm sure I looked strange, eyes glazed over, leaning forward, and sweaty, yet I felt electric, deciding that this full-body buzz, this clear-headed feeling, must be what an epiphany is like. From that day on, I eagerly awaited reading time, and, when we graduated to "independent reading," Miss Foster let me borrow the book. I devoured it. And the book after that, and the one after that.

Reading and writing never seemed like choices for me, and maybe that's why Rick Riordan's *Percy Jackson and The Olympians* series stayed in my consciousness. None of those characters had choices; they were born demigods, and despite their struggles, they all had divine destinies to fulfill. Percy Jackson's destiny was cleaning up after the Gods and trying to prevent a war, and my destiny lay in books. I'm aware it's pompous to compare my love for literature with a divine calling, but I've always known that working in the arts was what I was meant to do. I'm disabled, and as much as I liked to pretend that it never affected me, it did have a significant effect on my hobbies. Other children had difficulty striking up conversations with me. After all, they couldn't ask me to kick around a soccer ball or play jump rope, so when my sixth-grade teacher began to read Percy's story, I found refuge. I also found myself sliding down the slippery slope of becoming a semi-reclusive, gifted kid four grades above her reading level who refused to remove her nose from a book. That was a problem I had to deal with years later, in university, thrust back into a social world for six months before a pandemic tore it away. Books were my refuge then, too, and by that time I realized just how far I had strayed from my roots.

Let's flash back to the summer of 2015. I spent it indoors, practically tethered to my bed. I was about to begin high school, and I had stopped reading. I didn't notice at first: reading had always been part of my identity. But somehow, my favourite pastime slipped through the cracks after moving house in my eighth-grade year. Whenever I noticed a gap in time between books, I would brush it off and tell myself I'd read one when I got the chance. But I had ample time in my first years of high school. Sure, I was devoted to academics, but I had no friends. I mean that literally.

The few kids I hung around with transferred out of my school before the year was over, and because I put all my emotional eggs in one basket, I found myself alone for two years following the change. I was so frenzied by the changes in my social and academic setting that reading for fun didn't seem feasible. The only books I consistently read were the requisite Shakespeare (*Hamlet* was and still is a personal favourite) and Huxley's *Brave New World*, one of my most frequent re-reads. For all my self-proclaimed bookworm fervour, I didn't pick up a title that wasn't on a course outline for just under four years. I was so stressed about my future, my grades, and my lack of friends that reading for fun became a distraction from an all-important future. Little did I know, books would become a large part of that future. Near the end of high school, I discovered a love of writing.

Senior year, desperate for an elective to fill my schedule, I found an online creative writing class and signed up. Those months were my most prolific writing period — at least until I entered university and found a group of equally enthusiastic writers who pushed me to stretch my creative muscles (and my wrist, lest I develop carpal tunnel). During this semester of writing, seven years after I first opened Riordan's novel, my dad fell seriously ill. Together with academic pressure and teen angst, my family situation made expressing my feelings incredibly difficult. So, as an artsy teenager does, I wrote a poem. It was my first serious poem, a heartfelt expression of my inner turmoil, and you might expect me to be embarrassed by it in hindsight, but I'm not, partly because writing it was integral to my healing process, and partly because I lost that poem somewhere in the bowels of computer hell, in an old thumb drive, never to be found again. (I do remember getting an excellent grade on it, though.)

University rekindled my love of reading: a passion I never truly lost, just misplaced and found in a cardboard box on a mild summer day. The new house was empty. The echo was spooky even in broad daylight, especially in a 101-year-old farmhouse buzzing with flies that had taken a wrong turn from the nearby farm. The weather was so perfect that I was annoyed that I had to spend the day unpacking. I hadn't read for fun in years but had (and have) this magpie urge to collect things, including *many* books. I always unpack my books first, because disorganized space brings insomnia. While rooting through bulky boxes, I came across the *Percy Jackson and The Olympians* series carefully packed in paper. To protect the paperbacks from folds and dents, I'd placed them at the top of the pile. A pang of nostalgia every time I hold these books overcomes me, as though I'm eleven again, ready to jump into a familiar fantasy world. They're *so* comfortable that I took the second book to my first (and only) sleepaway camp and read it six times, and even brought a cheap paperback so I wouldn't worry about damaging my favourite copy. Always careful with books (a habit broken since university taught me annotation), I was extremely cautious with Percy Jackson.

I've kept those original novels for eleven years and three moves, and I'll have them with me until either they or I fall apart. They're an escape from the world and a doorway into it. They remind me *why* I spend my days reading and writing. I often lie awake at night contemplating what might've become of me if that teacher hadn't taken the time to read us *The Lightning Thief*. Would a different book now have me in its clutches? Or would I have wandered down a different path?

My book collection has grown around those original five *Percy Jackson* novels, and I couldn't be happier, although my wallet could be. And I worry about the structural integrity of my bookshelves, but I'll deal with that when the wood bends. I inhaled Rick Riordan's books as a child, and my nostalgic shrine continues to grow as he continues to publish. My taste *has* matured a bit, but nobody is too old for good old-fashioned whimsy, so I occasionally feed the fiery childhood fascination *The Lightning Thief* ignited with other mythological novels. Traces of Riordan's influence are in my writing. I giggle at the thought that a middle-grade book I read at eleven years old has had such a profound butterfly effect on my life. Maybe "Pegasus effect" would be more apt.

It would be disingenuous to suggest that my desire to craft gripping stories formed slowly. At eleven, I knew what an epiphany felt like. I needed to read and discovered that I needed to write. My tastes have darkened, and my current projects reflect that evolution, but what could've been darker to an eleven-year-old upon opening a novel than a promise of death? *The Lightning Thief* will follow me for the rest of my life; or, more accurately, I will follow it wherever it takes me.

Life is scary, and, often, there's no looking back — Percy taught me that. I found the most creative, caring group of people possible thanks to one little passage in the book that would push me headlong into life. Rick Riordan warned me to stop reading if I saw myself in his pages, but my only option was to push forward and forge a path of my own — and that meant diving in deeper, despite his cautionary plea.

The Sweet of Life

CHRISTINA WIENDELS

And freed from intricacies, taught to live,
The easiest way, nor with perplexing thoughts
To interrupt the sweet of life, from which
God hath bid dwell far off all anxious cares,
And not molest us, unless we our selves
Seek them with wandering thoughts, and notions vain.

(*Paradise Lost* by John Milton)

In the eighth or ninth line of a sonnet, there is a critical moment called a *volta* — Italian for "turn" — often indicated by a "But," "Yet," or "And yet." This pivot signals the possibility of transformation, or the introduction of an emotion or thought that reframes the preceding lines. Life, like the poetry I parse daily for my doctoral research, has a habit of suddenly changing shape. In 2020, my path was supposed to change. And it did, but not as I had expected.

That winter I eagerly awaited a major turn. My plans involved completing my Doctor of Philosophy in English, becoming a sessional instructor, and travelling for conferences. I was going to be happy — so I hoped. However, that March, an unexpected swerve thwarted my designs. The *volta* that rocked my world came in the form of a global pandemic. Would the university close? Would I be teaching my spring course online? How could I adapt the curriculum in a mere three weeks? What about conferences, which I needed for professional development? The COVID-19 outbreak would provoke what Ariel in William Shakespeare's *The Tempest* calls a "sea-change."

2020 ushered in not only masks, disappointment, and trepidation, but also waves of change that rippled through communities, cultures, and nations. I saw them, felt them, and read about them every day. People were writing about anxiety openly. They were even writing anxiously. For at least a year, almost every email ended with the warning "stay safe." I appreciated those words, but what would they do to us in the long run? The English word "anxious" derives partly from the Latin term *angere*, "to choke," and it was only a few weeks before fear had a chokehold on me. Between my students' qualms about online learning, my own doubts about teaching to a screen of faceless names, and my profound concern about a world already topsy-turvy with geological uncertainties, I found myself drowning in worries. Sea turtles were now ingesting disposable face masks in addition to microplastics and marine debris.

Occasionally, however, a heartening piece of news would surface to assuage my rattled nerves. One morning, I opened my laptop with trembling hands and an all-too-familiar sinking sensation. To my surprise, a headline for a popular article lifted my spirits: the rapid plunge in European tourism led to crystal-clear waters in Venetian canals, where fish could be seen swimming. The world seemed to be facing backward and forward simultaneously, and I was unsure which way it would roll. This virus, as it turned out, had not only physical but also mental effects, and I doubt anyone went untouched. I remember how not being able to see my students' faces made my heart sink. Yet, it steadied like an anchor gaining hold when their voices rang through my screen. Teaching online felt like pressing my ear up against a seashell: my students' voices carried echoes of a far-off yet familiar ocean.

No longer trusting the future, I found solace in poetry. Midway through English 1F03E, "The Written World," we were reading selections from Milton's *Paradise Lost*, the subject of my dissertation, and I was astonished by the aptness of several lines. I had read those verses many times, but they had never resonated personally until this moment. I scrambled for my pencil, circled phrases with a heavy loop, and wrote "ANXIETY!" in the margin. Then, I sat completely still, childlike with my legs crossed on a plush rug, and I began to cry. How did Milton identify mental illness in 1667? After that initial surprise, I felt neither happy nor sad, but understood and comforted — as though Raphael had been speaking not only to Adam, but also to me. The father of humanity was pointing out the essentials for a peaceful and pleasant life — fundamentals trampled in a fast-paced, accelerated world afflicted by illness and injury. Adam says to Raphael,

> freed from intricacies, taught to live,
> The easiest way, nor with perplexing thoughts
> To interrupt the sweet of life, from which
> God hath bid dwell far off all anxious cares,
> And not molest us, unless we our selves
> Seek them with wandering thoughts, and notions vain.

Adam's pairing of the words "anxious" and "cares" showed me that my anxiety was a way of *caring* — but for the wrong things. While neglecting the present moment, my weary mind had invested precious energy in ruminating about a future I could neither predict nor understand. Adam's words are physically nourishing; they call us to feed our bodies in a real, tangible way. However, these lines also urge us to replenish our minds. How can anyone think clearly or creatively with an intellect plagued by uneasiness? Anxiety can unsettle the easiest of lives. These verses reminded me that I do not need permission to slow down — that there is nothing unproductive or selfish about tasting life's simple pleasures.

When I envision my sweetest life, my mind drifts to abstract objectives such as happiness. Thus, I tend to overlook the concrete precursors to pleasure, staples of everyday life such as wholesome food and restorative rest. Adam chooses his words carefully. Rather than "the sweet life" (*la dolce vita*), he says, "the sweet *of* life." With that tiny preposition, he shifts focus away from a lost state of paradisiacal happiness and towards the indulgences available in a postlapsarian world.

Adam's "happy state" emerges from the alliterative quartet, "retire," "respite," "repast," and "repose" — diction strangely reminiscent of the contemporary maxim "R and R" or "rest and relax." As this enduring wisdom suggests, humans must refresh themselves continually. Adam's words guided me back to eating meals slowly, taking long, bubbly baths, and listening to nature's songs on my patio. "Freed from intricacies," I realized that happiness springs from acts of care.

Milton's proto-psychology reminds me of contemporary holistic healing practices. I'm thinking of mindfulness, meditation, and yoga, activities in which we slow, reflect, and re-orient ourselves to the present. COVID-19 forced our bodies to sit still and minds to speed up, and this tension between inert bodies and overactive minds persists. For me, "moving forward" means not only making peace with uncertainty, but also caring for a restless mind. From Adam, I learned to break patterns of thought that limit joy to productivity. I also learned that, to enhance my mood and well-being, I need to rest more rather than less. Raphael resolves Adam's doubts by teaching him that life *should* be simple — as easy as rhythmic breaths or lapping waves.

My pencil looped around the phrase, "unless we our selves / Seek them." Humans possess a kind of passive agency, a capacity to strive toward rest rather than productive activity. William Wordsworth, an admirer of Milton, called this aptitude a "wise passiveness." To sustain his God-given happiness, Adam must orient himself toward a pastoral uselessness — a self-preserving refusal to sacrifice the present to the future. The sibilance of the line, "And not molest us, unless" hissed as I read it aloud, forcing a serpent from my lips. Just as Satan denies God's love for him, we can harm ourselves unwittingly. When I lacked control over what lay ahead, Milton's Adam reminded me to live in the present and cultivate health, happiness, and inner peace. Free from fear, thought can fill even the most blank, uncertain future with possibility vast as the sea.

VII – ACCEPTANCE

The Bliss of Insignificance

KAATJE KEMPE

I had my first existential crisis at seven years old. I woke up sobbing, utterly convinced I was doomed for Hell because my parents weren't taking me to church. This panic was initiated by a few good friends of mine who, swinging on the monkey bars at recess, informed me of my terrible fate if I did not take immediate action. Thus, I was quite distraught. Luckily for me, my parents had an easy solution: we would attend church on Sundays.

After my first service, I thought, "Wow, I would rather spend an eternity in Hell than sit through another hour of that." The priorities of my seven-year-old self were questionable. The damage was done, however. My parents had resolved to attend church every Sunday from then on, despite my pleas to let me burn. Grappling with the knowledge of my inevitable doom at age seven was the first time in my life I feared death, but it was not the last.

The older I got, the more sceptical I became about religion; at age eleven, I decided Santa was definitely not real, and neither was God. I had too many unanswered questions and had suffered too many losses to believe there was anyone looking out for me. Every time I presented the Church with a question about God, I was met with the same response: "Trust in the Lord, for only He knows everything." I resolved to embrace an atheist existence. Now, the only problem was the crippling fear of eternal darkness and nothingness. By the time I hit puberty, I'd already wondered if my existence was meaningless, if there was any life after death, and if there was any point in living.

Even now, sharing a fear of death with most of my generation, I'm violently aware of my own mortality. We're told youth is wasted on the young and constantly made aware that the decisions we make now will dictate the rest of our lives. We exist in an age of social media and comparison — a fast-paced society that glorifies youth and discards the old. Since birth I have been running, always running, unaware of what I'm running towards and why, terrified I will be burying the dreams of my youth very soon; not yet 20, I'm already mourning the years I haven't lived.

With these thoughts stalking my mind, as a very confused and desperate person, I stumbled across Anita Diamant's *The Red Tent*. Browsing through an old bookshop, I first noticed the novel my friend had recommended so highly and couldn't see any harm in purchasing a second-hand copy for five dollars. Looking back, I wonder how different my outlook on life would be if I'd never spent that money.

Revolving around Dinah, daughter of Jacob, *The Red Tent* is a fictional retelling of a neglected society of biblical women and their lives. After a summer spent absorbing its brilliance word by word, I came across a line describing death as a source of gratitude, sympathy, and art rather than an enemy. I re-read those words a hundred times before beginning to understand what they were trying to tell me.

My biggest fear in life was dying, so the idea of death being anything other than my enemy seemed impossible. Diamant did not leave me alone to grapple with this concept. In *The Red Tent*, Dinah is constantly overcoming terrible losses: first, her beloved husband, and then, her only son. The pain nearly destroys her, until she realizes that without death, life would be devoid of meaning.

Death is the foundation of gratitude, because someone with an eternity to live cannot be thankful for life's fleeting moments. Death reminds people that life is short, and that every second is a gift. Death is humbling, which is why it's the foundation of sympathy. Every creature on this planet is commanded by death. We march to the grave side by side, no one superior to the tragedy. A person above death would be so removed from the world that time would slowly drain their heart of sympathy and compassion, leaving it empty, numb.

Death isn't our enemy but our ally, desperately fighting to save us from the cruelty of time.

Diamant's other claim (that death is the foundation of art) has taken on a special meaning now that I'm engaged in the creative process. Death inspires incredible emotions, which are then materialized by an artist's burning passion to understand, share, and manage those feelings. The motivation to capture life's beauty in a painting, poem, or sculpture stems from the knowledge that existence is brief and the desire to prolong it by any means possible. Eventually, even art must bow to death, but not before it outlives its artist. The best artists in the world are always revisiting death and thanking him for his service.

I'm not sure whether *The Red Tent* intends to paint existence as completely and utterly meaningless, but that's how I interpret it after spending so much time seeking a purpose, that I didn't realize death *is* what gives life purpose. To overcome a fear of death, I have to embrace it with open arms and to accept existence as blissfully meaningless and unimportant. Once I accept that I'm no more special than the person beside me, or the bumblebees, or the summer trees, I finally take my place in nature and shake this immense pressure to find meaning. Paradoxically, life is meaningful because it is not. I have no grander purpose for living than to experience the phenomenon of being alive: to taste, smell, feel, hear, and move as much as I can, to revel in my amazing, blissful insignificance, before death reclaims me. *The Red Tent* gave me permission to stop running, to slow down, and to appreciate the brief moments of being alive.

Diamant finishes with a baffling assertion. Diamant suggests that only love is not indebted to death. The most powerful force in *The Red Tent* is love, not because it is superior to death, but because they are equal. Dinah learns that love and death create the perfect balance in life, with neither owing the other a thing. Love is the purest of all life's pleasures, all-consuming and unaffected by time. Like death, love encourages intense emotions, both good and bad. In *The Red Tent*, love is the only sentiment worth dying for. There is nothing Dinah wouldn't do to protect her family, especially her child. Essentially, death and love create the push and pull forces of our world; a life full of love can greet the grave calmly.

What I also love about Diamant's adage is that it's open to interpretation, and my understanding of it changes regularly. At first, I thought Diamant was claiming that love lost to death is an injustice. Thus, love is not indebted to death, for love doesn't require death's services to remain pure. However, even the most painful losses provide perspective, growth, and intense human emotion. I now see death and love as partners filling human existence with meaning and purpose. Each force pulls at the human heart in a manner that demands to be felt and experienced.

My seven-year-old self wouldn't understand a word I'm saying, but she'd be happy to know I realize the worth of my existence. Whenever I read *The Red Tent*, I'm reminded that the value of life cannot be measured. Embracing the bliss of insignificance releases me from the pressures of purpose. If there are purposes, I choose them: to love, laugh, fight, cry, dream, and run. I choose to marvel at the vastness of life and to bask in my inconsequential role in the universe.

My Miracle

EMMA SEMPLE

But my miracle was different. My miracle was this: out of all the houses in all the subdivisions in all of Florida, I ended up living next door to Margo Roth Spiegelman.

(*Paper Towns* by John Green)

When a friend recommended *Paper Towns*, my first thought was, "great, another John Green novel about a manic-pixie-dream-girl." The term "manic-pixie-dream-girl" was coined by film critic Nathan Rabin to describe a stock character "exist[ing] solely in the fevered imaginations of sensitive writer-directors to teach broodingly soulful young men to embrace life and its infinite mysteries and adventures." In other words, she's the vehicle by which male protagonists develop, and I have always hated her. Yet, it's not her fault: how is a character who exists solely to bolster another character's story going to be anything but one-dimensional? I hesitated to waste my time on such a novel, because I was still recovering from another John Green bestseller, *The Fault in our Stars* — not to say I didn't enjoy it. It's just that the manic-pixie-dream-girl (in male form) was so distracting that I had a hard time appreciating the heartfelt love story. Needless to say, it was a while before I picked up *Paper Towns*. When I finally did, Margo Roth Spiegelman was a pleasant surprise.

The novel begins predictably. Quentin, "Q" for short, waxes

philosophical about how everyone gets a miracle, and his is living next door to Margo Roth Spiegelman. I almost put the book down right then. Possessed by some unseen force, however, I continued, and I'm glad I did. I was happy to reach the third chapter, our first subtle glimpse at Margot's imperfections. As Q gushes about her, he admits, "she never really asked me questions, so the only way to avoid silence was to keep her talking." This observation was out of place, and it caught me off-guard. Was he aware of her unlikeable qualities? Was he… annoyed? This incongruous comment is the first of several humanizing moments. Later, Margo runs away and leaves behind a series of clues about her destination. Diligently following her bread-crumbs, Q learns plenty of new information about his neighbour, much of which challenges his idealistic perception of her. Ironies build into a beautiful climax as he deciphers her hints and trails her to the paper town of Agloe, New York. When he arrives, Margo is upset, because she doesn't want to be found. A fight ensues, and she cries, "You're not even pissed at me, Q! You're pissed at this idea of me you keep inside your brain from when we were little!"

When I read this dialogue, I screamed, "Yes!" in the middle of my hushed, underused high school library. It was the first time I'd encountered the manic-pixie-dream-girl trope being challenged, and I was ecstatic. Here was a seemingly perfect character, adored by this boy because of his erroneous impression, telling him flat-out that he's wrong. Infuriated by everyone's expectations, she longs to escape the box of her life. Margo wishes not to be placed on a pedestal, but rather to be exactly who she is: selfish, eccentric, annoying, and wonderfully flawed.

Margo Roth Spiegelman gave me the permission I didn't know I needed to write deeply flawed characters. My creativity flourished thanks to her and her imperfections. No longer would I limit myself to archetypes or force my characters into simplistic boxes. The first character I wrote after *Paper Towns* was April. Not quite fitting any mould, she has yet to appear in a larger project. The most important quality I gave her was a flaw yet not a particularly horrendous or huge shortcoming: nail-biting. But that choice led me to wonder, "Why would she bite her nails?" and "Has she ever tried to stop biting her nails?" and "Is stopping part of her character arc?" These inquiries might seem trivial, yet they are precisely the types of musings that deepen characters. This line of questioning led me to discover that April is anxious and has poor impulse control, traits that get her into a lot of trouble.

While I'm still not a proponent of the manic-pixie-dream-girl trope, Margo changed how I read and write stories. Her biggest flaw is her narcissism. No one sees her depth, so she spends her time peering into it. She's afraid when Q tries to see her authentic self, and that fear drives her into isolation. Yet, she emerges as a whole person the moment Q's picture-perfect mental image falls away. In the twenty remaining pages, Q realizes that the magical Margo of his childhood is as illusory as the enigmatic runaway who left a trail of clues in her wake. What's real is a flawed and eccentric girl on the brink of a new beginning. His closing words aptly summarize this revelation: "Yes, I can see her almost perfectly in the cracked darkness." Quirky characters like Margo urge us to start new lives — as artists and as humans.

Perfectly Ordinary

KRISTYN HICK

Truthfully, this story ends with me still sitting on the floor of my room won-dering who I'll become if I leave this town and remembering when I was a little kid and how I loved to fall asleep in my bed breathing in the smell of freshly cut grass and listening to the voices of my sister and my mother talking and laughing in the kitchen and the sounds of my dad poking around in the yard, making things beautiful right outside my bedroom window.

(*A Complicated Kindness* by Miriam Toews)

I first read Miriam Toews's breakout novel as part of my M.A. studies. When I was drowning in Dickens's *Bleak House* and Eliot's *Adam Bede,* a mandatory Canadian Literature course put *A Complicated Kind-ness* on my plate. At first, I admit, I was drawn to it because of its easy prose and shorter length. A welcome relief! But soon, I was caught up in Nomi's many misadventures.

I was the second in my family to pursue a university education and the first to venture into Graduate Studies. Every day of my M.A., I reveled in the pursuit of higher learning, yet many of the classics felt far away from my own experiences as a child and youth. I loved them for that distance. Literature was one of the only ways for me to experience worlds vastly different from mine; the cobblestone streets of nineteenth-century London seemed remote and unreachable to a small-town Ontario child.

The desire to be great, to stand apart, to excel was ingrained in me during my schooling. The pressure of academia and the familiar monster of imposter syndrome often loomed while I tried to write essays and prepare for seminars. Through all of Nomi's heartbreaks in the novel, she should be discouraged, beaten down. And she is. Nomi isn't a brilliant academic or force of political or societal change; she is a broken teenager. Still, she is a lovable character worthy of attention, and her story is poignant, compelling, and beautiful.

In the sentence of *A Complicated Kindness*, excerpted above, I saw my world intersect with the universe of great storytelling. The sound of my father cutting the grass hugged me with nostalgia. In the laughter of Nomi's sister and mother in the kitchen, I heard the echoes of my happy childhood home and smelled my mother's homemade muffins baking.

We grew up on the family dairy farm beside my grandparents' house. As a child, I ran barefoot over the lawn that separated our houses to barge in on my grandparents and pester them with endless questions and demands for cookies. My memories of the long, seemingly endless days of childhood involve aimlessly chattering with my grandparents about their favourite sweet treats, wondering how hummingbirds could move their wings so fast, and questioning why the rosary couldn't be worn as a necklace. The beads were so pretty! It certainly didn't occur to me to ask if my grandparents were busy, but they never rushed my meandering visits. Buzzing with energy, I couldn't be persuaded to stay too long, but my Grandpa never failed to call out, "Come again Krissy!" as I breezed from the room, likely without so much as a goodbye. After all, my next visit was imminent, either later that day or the next. My grandparents never ventured far from the farm, so my memories of them are largely confined to a dated old farmhouse. But with the sepia of nostalgia, these prosaic memories are more and more magical.

My other grandparents purchased a family cottage when my oldest sister was born. Every long weekend of the summer months and for a week or two in August, the cottage became our home: a place where aunts, uncles, cousins, and pets gathered, or, more accurately, crammed. The dress code was sweatpants and bathing suits. The only entertainment was a TV that got three channels, if we were lucky enough to turn the dial to *just* the right spot. But, for the most part, television was forgotten in favour of swimming, campfires, intense games of cribbage or euchre, and waterskiing. If anyone happened to suggest they might want to go fishing later, they would find Grandpa tinkering away in the basement attaching lures and fixing reels to ensure casting was buttery smooth. He worked quietly all day, even if the original suggestion was lost to other excitements of the moment. As long as we were happy and busy, he was content as a silent observer. In the final moments of *A Complicated Kindness*, my parents, grandparents and their extraordinarily ordinary lives suddenly became the centerpiece of hope in a novel — a first in my reading experience. Parents, unexceptional for their dutiful daily drudgery of chores mixed with laughter and love, were the heroes of the story. It was an idea that seemed revolutionary to me.

The ending of the novel is hopeful. True, Nomi remains on her bedroom floor, paralyzed by the unknown of her future. However, her final thought is about her parents who show their love through the most ordinary and mundane activities. And yet, this love is so powerful that just the memory of it, when Nomi is left alone, is enough to give her hope. Now that I've become a parent, I want to protect my kids from all the sharp edges of the world. We work so hard as parents to baby-proof everything — cover the corners of coffee tables, install gates on stairs, put covers over electrical outlets. I think these actions are to reassure ourselves that we can protect our children from the hidden dangers of life — a false hope, of course. This book reminds me that extreme safety measures may not be necessary. Our love for our children will resurface in their memories as the smell of onion and garlic while I'm cooking my special spaghetti sauce, the feel of a late-night cuddle after a nightmare invaded their dreams, and the giggles of their siblings during a silly dance in the living room. I hope when my kids look back on their childhood, they think of our annual tradition of driving to a nearby town's Christmas light display, our Saturday morning puzzle sessions, and baking cookies. I hope when they are lonely and scared, they remember us blasting Imagine Dragons' "Thunder" to try and drown out the unnerving cracks of summer storms. I hope they realize that in all these endeavors to make life beautiful outside their bedroom windows, they see that a simple, ordinary, and tragic world is the most beautiful world.

Falling in Love

MEGAN SHANNON

After all, what is love but understanding?

(*A Lady for a Duke* by Alexis Hall)

There is no single literary work that has changed my life. I have no stories about a eureka moment, or an emotional awakening, or a single book that altered the course of my life. There's no text to pinpoint because every work of literature I've ever loved has changed my life in some way. At twenty-six years old, I don't know where I end and books begin, or where books end, and I begin.

The first time I felt a soul-deep connection with a book, I was three or four years old, visiting my grandparents at their summer house. I spent most of my afternoon "quiet time" — my mom's big-kid alternative for naptime — playing librarian in front of the small bookshelf in my room. I spent hours pulling out hardcovers, pretending I was taking them from an archive and blowing plumes of dust off their old jackets. Of all the books on the shelf, I was drawn to one in particular: *The Adventures of Johnny Chuck* by Thornton Burgess. Every time I sat in front of that shelf, something about that book pulled me in. It felt *right* in my hands, and I never wanted to put it down. It was a smallish hardcover book, just a little bigger than a mass market paperback, in a burnt orange colour, with my dad's name in faded ink on the inside. Carried around for the rest of my visit with my Grandparents, that book became an extension of myself. Suddenly, I felt important and grown up, more complete somehow, simply because I had this book in my hand or tucked under my arm.

On the long drive home, I spent three full hours flipping through the pages of *Johnny Chuck* in what I thought was an award-winningly convincing performance of A Girl Who Can Read. I even went so far as to tell my mom what was going on in the book whenever she asked me. I made up entire plotlines and worlds based on the single black-and-white illustration in each chapter, and I was deeply invested in the woven tales. What I didn't realize until many years later was that my mom knew *Johnny Chuck* was above my reading level. She didn't buy my performance for one second, but she continued to ask me about the book whenever she saw me with it (which was every day until I could read the words and realized the plot of the novel paled in comparison to the version I'd fabricated). She understood what the book meant to me and the importance of encouraging my imagination.

This attitude is exactly what Alexis Hall means when he says, "after all, what is love but understanding?" in *A Lady for a Duke*, a romance novel I love. Within context, this quotation is about the understanding between romantic partners, but for me, those words describe both my personal relationships, and my relationship with literature as well. When I pulled *The Adventures of Johnny Chuck* off my grandparents' bookshelf, I fell in love for the first time, and this love irrevocably changed who I am and how I find connection with literature. When the right book comes along, you feel it with your whole chest. A good book squeezes your heart and weaves its way through your veins until it becomes part of you, helping you grow and change while your imagination runs wild, just as any kind of love alters who you are. My mom understood this type of love when she asked me to summarize the plot of a book I couldn't yet read. The question was her quiet way of saying, *I see you, and I see the way your love for this book could alter your life, if cultivated and encouraged.* After all, what is love but understanding that one does not need to be able to read all the words to be led by a book, or to love it in return?

Like my four-year-old self, I tend to carry around the books and quotations that changed my life wherever I go — never anywhere without a book in my hand or my bag. But I also carry literature around in my head and my heart, because if I love a story, it becomes embedded in who I am. I might never have figured out that I'm bisexual if I hadn't taken a queer literature class in the fourth year of my B.A. and found pieces of my own feelings scattered across every book we read, and I don't think I'd have started keeping a journal if I hadn't read *The Princess Diaries* and been inspired by Mia Thermopolis.

Thanks to my love of Meg Cabot's words and the kindred spirit I found in Mia as a young girl, journaling became an outlet for my thoughts and feelings, and provided me with a place to tell the story of my own life. However, my journal is also a sort of chapbook for collecting the quotes I come across while reading that impact me most—the sentences that stop me in my tracks and play through my brain like a catchy song in idle moments. When I began working on this project, the first thing I did was turn to the quotes I've collected over the last decade of my life to see what stories they could tell. Would they be able to put my relationship to literature into the words I had not yet been able to find?

As I flipped through old journals and read through pages and pages of foraged words, I realized that this collection of quotes was my way of puzzling together parts of myself I could feel but found impossible to describe. The line "his hugs were her favorite, solid and strong and never halfway" in akwaeke emezi's *Pet* described how I like to be hugged but also how to hug others. Hugs are one of the best ways to give someone else a little piece of how much you love them, and you never know how badly someone needs that love. The words, "once, one of us fell asleep reading and afterwards explained, 'I often get tired when I'm learning a lot'" in Eve Kosofsky Sedgwick's *Touching Feeling,* remind me that learning is a daily challenge: it can deplete me, even while filling me with knowledge. If the academics and feminists that I look up to grow tired when learning new things, I should be kind to myself when drained by how much and how quickly I'm expected to learn as a graduate student. The quotation, "hospitals were kind of like airports — sad airports — full of distilled time and echoes," enchanted me when I was reading Alexis Hall's *How to Blow it With a Billionaire,* because I didn't expect a queer romance novel I read in 2023 to make sense of how I felt about hospitals at age twelve when my grandmother was dying of cancer and I spent every weekend visiting her.

When I first started questioning my sexuality, I wasn't fully aware that the books from my queer lit class had set off that particular avalanche of feelings. At the time, I was recovering from a broken heart and had thrown myself into my schoolwork as a distraction. Truthfully, my sexuality was the farthest thing from my mind. Even the quotes I collected from the queer literature I was reading are not about sexuality at all, but instead about the characters' own relationships with literature and with themselves. From Virginia Woolf's *Orlando,* I copied, "once the disease of reading has laid upon the system it weakens it so that it falls an easy prey to that other scourge which dwells in the inkpot and festers the quill. The wretch takes to writing." Again, from Alexis Hall's *How to Blow It With a Billionaire,* I copied, "sometimes life was shitty, and the people you loved were hurting, and sad and scared and lonely were what you had to feel." I now understand why I was drawn to these novels: my queerness, and the queerness of the characters and the authors who created them, are tightly woven with a love for literature. I saw myself reflected in these queer characters and thus began reflecting on myself. After all, what is love but understanding that sometimes novels can see you better than you see yourself?

By the fourth year of my B.A., I'd spent years reading queer theory and innumerable hours discussing the intersections of gender and sexuality. But not one of these theoretical texts guided my journey of self-discovery. Not one of them got into my veins and made me feel seen as queer novels did. The way fictional characters described love and literature reminded me of that feeling I got as a kid carrying around a burnt-orange hardcover. Suddenly, the world made a little more sense and was a little less lonely. "There are some things you can only see through tears," writes Jordy Rosenberg in *Confessions of the Fox,* and I think being heartbroken when I read those books allowed me to see myself reflected in the magical queerness of loving litera-ture and to assemble the pieces of a self.

Years later, after reading hundreds of queer lit books and coming out as bisexual, I stumbled upon the quotation, "after all, what is love but understanding," in *A Lady for a Duke* by Alexis Hall. This sentence shaped and made sense of the way I understood love. It is understand-ing someone else and being understanding *of* them. In every romance novel I've ever read, the protagonists realize they are in love because the person they are with (whether that be because of a marriage of convenience, a fake relationship, or a sex pact that wasn't supposed to involve feelings) understands them in a way no one else ever has. They often have such a deep connection that they can see hidden parts of one another, and they love each other anyway. Romance novels show readers, through the inevitable third act breakup, that people are flawed and make mistakes without meaning to. What makes the relationship work out in the end is understanding the beloved when they make mistakes and giving them the space to do so.

This, I think, is the reason my first experience of falling in love was with books. People have not always made sense to me. Social anxiety and shyness, especially as a child, made it hard for me to find deep connections with others. I often tripped over my feelings because I didn't understand how to express them. Much later in life I realized my loneliness for other kinds of love than familial. Literature never pressured me to squish myself into a box to fit in, nor did it force me into awkward, embarrassing conversations. As soon as I picked up a book or walked into the public library, an immense calm washed over me, no longer lonely or afraid; I was simply a girl, sitting in front of a book, asking it to love her. Every evening throughout my childhood, in bed with a book and a flashlight under my pillow, I would stay up past my bedtime to read in secret. In that sense, books were not only my first love, but also my first nighttime tryst, and thus a partner in the romance of life.

After all, what is love but understanding that ink on paper can queer my understanding of myself and the world around me? There's no way magic isn't real when a novel written over a hundred years ago introduced me to one of my best friends in the world, simply because she noticed when I pulled it out during class. "How do you feel about *The House of Mirth*?" Emma asked me. "I'm presenting on it next week and I'm not a fan." I responded that surprisingly I was enjoying it, sparking a conversation that continues today, five years later, all thanks to Edith Wharton.

Which book will change your life? Pick one up and begin reading. When a book knows you need it, it'll find its way into your hands and become part of who you are. That's the magic, and why literature leads to love.

Emma and I

LISA KOVAC

The very sight of Mrs. Weston, her smile, her touch, her voice was grateful to Emma, and she determined to think as little as possible of Mr. Elton's oddities, or of anything else unpleasant, and enjoy all that was enjoyable to the utmost.

(*Emma* by Jane Austen)

I was probably too young for Jane Austen's *Emma* the first time I read it: the purportedly appealing romantic entanglements left my twelve-or-thirteen-year-old self unimpressed. To be fair to my former self, the purportedly appealing romantic entanglements still leave me largely unimpressed, so maybe the mismatch was less between the book and my age than between the book and my nascent notions about characters and what's best for them.

I picked *Emma* up because her name was the title. Many children's books I loved had titles composed of eponyms and epithets. There were *Anne of Green Gables*, *The Hobbit*, *A Little Princess*, and *Harry Potter and the Philosopher's Stone*. While I didn't always develop rapport with people in the so-called "real world," I loved the people I met in books. I was fascinated by how characters felt about and imagined their lives, how those emotions and imaginings helped or hindered their responses to others, how they met and parted and loved and hated. I longed to know more about how my favourite characters made friends, faced foes, and learned compassion. I wanted to write my own books, though I had vague misgivings that my take-them-or-leave-them approach to children my age made me experientially ill-equipped. Also, I wanted to read everything I could get my hands on, and started my literary education with *Emma*.

Emma Woodhouse seems quite satisfied with her life, if a little at loose ends upon the departure of her just-married governess. The loss of Miss Taylor's constant company leaves Emma with a void, which she plans to fill by playing matchmaker. This scheme annoyed me: of all possible pastimes at her disposal — not to mention all the ways she could use her time and wealth and influence to do real good — why would Emma choose to meddle in other people's relationships? Besides, as little as I cared for romantic plots, I recognized that Harriet Smith loved Robert Martin, and that Emma's motives in separating the prospective lovers were self-interested and classist. Why read about a character who made a hobby of rearranging other people's lives to suit her own ends? Villains, not heroines, were supposed to wreck lives. Tempted to drop the book, I slogged on in spite of myself.

Later in Volume One, Emma encounters some snags in her match-making machinations. Though she talks Harriet into loving Elton, his apparent interest in Harriet mysteriously wanes. Perplexed by her own uneasiness, Emma cheers up at the prospect of visiting her beloved Miss Taylor, now named Mrs. Weston, for there was:

Not any one, to whom she related with such conviction of being listened to and understood, of being always interesting and always intelligible, the little affairs, arrangements, per-plexities, and pleasures of her father and herself. This was a pleasure which perhaps the whole day's visit might not afford, which certainly did not belong to the present half-hour; but the very sight of Mrs. Weston, her smile, her touch, her voice was grateful to Emma, and she determined to think as little as possible of Mr. Elton's oddities, or of anything else unpleas-ant, and enjoy all that was enjoyable to the utmost.

Here, I did drop the book, not in disdain but in delight. Emma's determination to revel in the anticipated relief of seeing, touching and talking to one specific person was emotional terrain I knew by heart but had never noticed in a book.

I liked books better than people. Most adults read my characteristic solitude as cause for concern: they cross-questioned me about how few friends I had and hatched schemes for me to make more. I began to recoil from recess the way another child might shrink from math. My social alienation haunted me in the form of an inarticulable but persistent sense of unease, and I sometimes pondered whether I should alter myself to be more like my peers. I began to wonder whether other children left me to my own devices not amicably, as I'd believed, but disdainfully, because they perceived me as inadequate playmate material. If human relationships were this fraught with fault lines, how could I ever understand people enough to create credible characters? However, my sense of myself as somehow alien and doomed to fail always disintegrated in the presence of particular people — my best friend, my grandparents, my two beloved teachers — with whom I felt "always interesting and always intelligible" as I was, no revisions required.

I returned to *Emma*, and Emma returned to meddling in her friend's supposed best interests. My delight devolved into renewed revulsion: why was this miserable person still so determined to keep Harriet apart from Martin and marry her to Elton? Couldn't Emma tell that Elton was uninterested in Harriet? Emma was about to ruin the lives of people she claimed to like. She hadn't deserved that moment of basking in Mrs. Weston's nearness. Emma could "enjoy all that was enjoyable" after she let Harriet make her own choices. That was what any protagonist worth their salt would do.

However, Emma refuses to relent. When the Elton plan falls through, bafflement and contrition buffet her; she comforts Harriet but resents the endurance of her grief; for a few pages, she forswears matchmaking — until the next potential husband for Harriet comes along. Then, there is a new volume, and a new character enters Emma's world: Jane Fairfax, a longstanding but distant acquaintance.

Why does Emma resent Jane's talent on the pianoforte? Can't Emma just practise more? *How dare this shallow woman remind me of me!*

Fortunately, as I kept reading, I noticed happier similarities between me and Emma — affinities beyond our disinclination to practice piano, our growing awareness and unease about our incomplete understanding of others, or, more specifically, our discomfort, not with the distance between ourselves and other people, but with how others might find us wanting as a result of that distance. Emma's devotion to her doting father reminded me of the favouritism flourishing between me and my grandfather.

Perhaps this Emma person had a few things going for her. And yet, would she ever learn that manipulating people wasn't a viable career? Would she ever channel her charitable proclivities into doing any good? Would she ever shape up and become a heroine?

What is a heroine, anyway? Emma may not deserve her joy, but perhaps joy isn't always something we earn. Joy is something we snatch when we can, with or without the social skills to deserve it. I like reading about Emma as she is: sometimes well-meaning, sometimes snobbish, sometimes contrite, and sometimes determined to do what she wants without consulting anyone else involved. In the end, Emma muddles through without understanding the people she meets. Harriet's happy ending with Martin baffles Emma and leads to a cordial distance between the two friends; she clears the air with Jane Fairfax, but they also go separate ways. Emma retains three intimacies: her father, Mr. Knightley, and Mrs. Weston.

I decided to write about people like Emma: not heroes who do the right thing and are beloved by everyone, but people who sometimes feel like doing the right thing and keep doing it even when they've decided it might be the wrong thing. About people who know they don't understand others but search for ways to use their talents within their communities anyway, with the help of a few friends for whom they are "always interesting and always intelligible." I'm probably qualified to write flawed characters like Emma. Like me.

VIII – RESISTANCE

"tricky one, that story"

MONIKA LEE

───────────

Biindigen, namadabin, oowaah. good to see you. i'll get the tea. watch your feet. don't let that one nip you in the toes. gotta watch your feet with that one. he bark too much too. i'll get the tea. that'll start that story off good, gotta start that story off in the right direction because you don't want it going somewhere you don't want it to go. get into all kinds of trouble, that one. gotta keep a hold of that story. start it off right. like the way it happened. don't want it to start thinking it is all kinds of a big deal, big shot, that one. tricky one, that story.

(*Islands of Decolonial Love* by Leanne Betasomasake Simpson)

In 1982, I found myself beside Linda in a Shakespeare course taught by the famous Northrop Frye at the University of Toronto's Victoria College. Together, we were irreverent about the articulate Torontonian students with their command of critical discourse and their easy urban sophistication. We mocked them and the skinny teaching assistant named Lionel Puddlington for things over which they had no control: their pallor and their privilege. Together, we constructed an armour of mercilessness to shield ourselves from a sense of inferiority. Neither of us ever deigned to raise our hand to answer a question, and we roasted those who did as mere toadies and sycophants. Through satire, we constructed a flimsy simulacrum of superiority.

it's about audience. some audiences you got to lose your accent and use big english words. you think I can't use big english words? I'll show you. none of that stuff is important anyway. what is important is who is listening.[5]

Linda and I lived in the women's residence called Margaret Addison Hall among the self-titled Fourth-Floor Floozies, a group of women whose ribald humour struck me as obscene and whose escapades with the men's residence in the more attractive historical buildings called Burwash Hall were nothing short of dangerous. During Orientation Week, for example, while we were fast asleep, many drunken male strangers broke into our bedrooms at 3 a.m. and dragged us from our beds to throw us into the showers.

Like most Canadians, I grew up ignorant about the Indigenous peoples in my country. Only a few kilometres away from where I lived was Canada's largest reservation by population and second largest in area, and I never knew it was there. My parents were pro civil-rights activists who cared about social justice, attended protests, and sheltered American draft dodgers during the Vietnam War. We were not allowed to play "Cowboys and Indians" with our cousins, who thought we were weird, so we adapted the game into "Cats and Mice". My father frequently talked about adopting one of the young Indigenous boys advertised in the Hamilton Spectator on Saturdays. Dad wanted to help.

i worried therapy-lady was trying to assimilate me into a plasticy Christian that can stand in the middle of a car wreck and thank the heavenly father for the band aid they found in their purse.

My stunningly gorgeous, impeccably dressed, tough-talking Indigenous friend Linda tried to educate me. She had grown up on that huge and sprawling Haudenosaunee Six Nations Reserve of the Grand

---

5. All the italicized passages are from *Islands of Decolonial Love: Songs and Stories* published by Arbeiter Ring Publishing (2013) and copyright held by Leanna Betasamosake Simpson.

River so close to my family home, the one I'd never heard of. Like everyone on our residence floor, I had assumed Linda was white. One night, however, she graciously indulged my questions until 4 a.m., and she told me about her two nations (Mohawk and Cayuga), the Longhouse religion in which she'd been raised, her language, her real name, the lack of running water and plumbing inside their house, her huge collection of siblings and half-siblings. I was shocked to learn that she didn't consider herself Canadian. She talked about the territories of her people which extended south of the American border and how the border meant nothing to her.

i redrew the maps those old ones kept tucked away in their bones.

We bonded over shared secrets. She liked the Jewish boys best, because they understood better than anyone else. And they couldn't marry her any more than she could marry them.

Later, she told me about the day her father left when she was three years old, how she held onto his leg, how she cried and pleaded with him not to go, how he left anyway, how she would never forgive him, and how, when he died, she would claim her share of whatever money he had left his new family and his new children.

she sat inside the loss. she paced. she tried to travel. she paced in order to travel.

One day, she came to my residence room and asked to borrow $250, a huge sum of money for me at the time. She would pay it back in two weeks when she was paid. I knew that the loan had something to do with the mysterious events and people on the Six Nations Reserve but didn't ask questions. I gave her the loan and she returned it two weeks later.

some people didn't survive.
some people gave up. moved on. buried. forgot.
some people found ways to cope.

some people work hard at just breathing. just breathe.

One day, she told me almost casually that her alcoholic stepfather had sexually abused her growing up. I asked her if she had ever repressed the experience, because those were the days of a furor over "false memory syndrome." No, she'd never forgotten it and didn't think it was the kind of thing a person could forget, especially not when it happened regularly over a period of years. He was still married to her mother, and Linda still saw him every time she went back to the Reserve.

i knew that getting hit like that was supposed to be traumatic, so i acted like it was even though i actually didn't feel anything at all.
      you better not whine and cry and act like the world is going to end because it isn't. you're not the first person to go through this.

Everybody liked Linda — the other girls on our floor, her many friends, my various boyfriends, my sisters, my own friends, my parents, and my eventual husband. Her comic timing and witty banter entertained us, and her beauty shone, but it was her affectionate soul that consolidated my love. Despite her incessant and impermeable bravado, no beating heart was more tender.

i think vera's beautiful and I mostly just stare at her when she talks. her brown eyes are both piercing and full of warmth at the same time. she has freckles and dimples and long, shiny black hair. her skin is flawless, and her sarcasm cuts through all the bullshit, as she calls it.

We both did Honours degrees at the University of Toronto.
We both got good grades.
She was prettier than me.
She was more popular than me.
She was more ambitious and planned to go to medical school.
She worked harder. At everything.

kwe's mom taught her how to do everything because she'd need to know how to do everything. chop wood. light a fire. light your inner fire. keep it lit. blow on the embers. fan the flames. fire needs breath. life needs fire. breath feeds shkode.

Then, Linda and I each walked into the narratives which were already written, engraved on the sands of time before we were born. Out of loyalty to her family and her culture, she moved back to the reserve where she lived with her handsome partner, an architect, and their four gorgeous children.

———————

her mother died
her closest sister died at age 30 of a stroke
her baby died
the father of her children left her
she had major depressive disorder
she wanted to die

fuck, why was the universe trying to destroy you? why didn't you get some say? sometimes people's lives are just shit through no fault of their own and not even fucking oprah's cash and her tool box of privileged platitudes can fix it.

she got cancer
her son was arrested
she was arrested
there was a race riot (against her people) in Caledonia
her niece went to jail for drug dealing
the niece's baby was born addicted to heroin
Linda adopted him
she drove him to McMaster Medical Centre twice a day for heroin injections until he was drug-free

———————

One day, I received a beautiful letter from her expressing her gratitude for just sitting and crying with her over her dead baby boy John. She described the perfection of his wee limbs and the pathos of his tiny coffin.

One day, our all-night conversations marked by hilarity and tears ceased. I could cope with Linda, but not with myself, my complicity, my saviour complex, my guilt. We went silent.

you can hear silence if you try.

My adult daughter works in Pikangikum, the most Ojibway place on earth, a location which made headlines in 2005 for being the suicide capital of the world. They have food, water, and healthcare insecurity up there, and it's very cold. Last week, a child in Grade Six died by suicide.

land giving up truths.
skin made of someone else's shame.

When I discovered *Islands of Decolonial Love*, about different Indigenous nations and cultures than Linda's, I read and re-read it obsessively. A lifetime of watching the news, reading articles and books, and saying land acknowledgements hadn't explained a thing. The only way I could understand my friend and her experiences was through reading fiction.

Michi Saagiig Nishnaabeg writer Leanne Betasomasake Simpson's songs and stories break apart generic and linguistic conventions, and they challenge the very foundations of colonialism. They broke me open and shattered my lifelong assumptions into pieces. Linda first taught me how to listen, but these stories taught me how to hear what she had been saying all along. Fiction was my translator.

Knowing that I'm privileged and feeling the injustice of that fact are not the same thing. Not even close.

it was too much to ask of a white lady.

I picked up the phone.

Concrete NDN: Mr. Inadifferentway

SCOTTY OLSEN

W ho cares about a giant peach, some kid and his hatchet, or some stupid spider web in a barn? When I look back at my childhood, I remember how much I hated reading. My schooling was connected to reading in every way, and I would do anything to avoid it. I'd have friends tell me what happened, I'd cheat, I'd read every other page, I'd just read the first and last chapters, I'd watch the movie.

I never saw the point. I mean, I loved stories, but why were they forcing me to read these irrelevant ones? In primary school, they'd try to force me to read, and I'd demand to play. They'd want to expose me to new narratives, and I'd want to create my own. Their narratives were never as good as the ones in my head.

Then they sent me to special education, segregated me, and told me I was not good enough. Was I not good enough? Or was I in a classical education dumping ground for an Indigenous kid who was defiant in the classroom?

I worked my way out of special education, but by high school I was so resentful, bitter, and angry that I had a foot out the door already. I mean, why wouldn't I? This institution was just a form of assimilation with a new coat of paint. However, my grade ten high school English teacher said I had something, and she promised me that if I applied myself and worked hard, she'd put me in the advanced class the following year. She said I wasn't special; in fact, I was just like everyone else. Who would've thought that little bit of support would work so well? I finished her class and looked forward to the following year, for once.

Summer came, as it always did. I partied, got into some fights, caused some trouble, and home life became a bit problematic, but I was anticipating being in a class with a teacher who wanted me there, one who thought I was normal. A teacher who felt that I could stand with the others and meet expectations.

In the fall, they told me there was no room for me in that class. They told me that nothing could be done. I went back to not caring. My feet got closer to that door — to dropping out. Their alternative was a grade eleven English class with a teacher who had a reputation for being a pothead, for showing tons of movies, for passing kids who didn't do any work, and who never chased you down, sent you to the office, or fought with you.

Fine by me, I thought.

The semester went as planned. It started with movies, continued with movies, and finished with more movies. It was fun when the days lined up when the teacher actually took attendance and I actually attended. Then, one day, out of nowhere, Mr. Indifferent asked us to read. He said this was an amazing book. We asked if there was a movie. There wasn't. The book was *Angela's Ashes*. He said it was about a poor Irish Catholic kid's journey through the miserable lanes of Limerick. I was a poor concrete Indian kid living on North Edmonton's miserable 118th avenue. Why the hell would I care about what happens to some poor Irish Catholic kid? He explained that, to pass his class, we needed to read this book and write a report. I resisted. He insisted. He begged. I laughed. And this continued until the end of the year.

"You aren't going to complete this are you?" he said at the eleventh hour while scratching his 5 o'clock shadow.

"Fuck that," I said, with a laughter that mocked his efforts.

He took a long look at me. "What if I make you a deal?" He let out a sigh. "I pass you now, and you complete the report for me in your final year of high school," Mr. Indifferent said with reluctance in his voice.

"Absolutely," I said with a twinkling mischievousness.

Summer came, as it always did. I partied, got into more fights, caused more trouble, and home life became more problematic, but I was looking forward to finishing my time in that awful institution. When I returned for grade 12 and saw Mr. Indifferent in the halls, he'd ask when his report was getting done. I always replied, "soon." Eventually, it became a schtick, a real "who's on first" routine; he'd even laugh and smile when he asked. He knew the truth. He knew that he'd been hustled, and that I didn't plan to read that book. I was sick of the racism at the high school. You can only be called a "dirty fucking Indian" for so many years before deciding that there are better places in this world. So, I dropped out — walked out that door without looking back.

Years passed, flipping burgers. There were no summer holidays, but I still partied, still fought, still caused trouble, and home was still problematic. Then, one day, I was shuffling through a pile of discount DVDs at HMV and I saw it there, for four dollars: a gray image of a young Irish boy's face and a title in bright yellow, *Angela's Ashes*. I thought to myself, *you know what? I'll pick up this movie and give it a watch for ol' Mr. Indifferent. I owe him that much for giving me a break.* The opening lines of the movie punched me in the face.

A miserable childhood, filthy poverty, and finding a way to survive.

Andrew Bennett's voice imprinted itself as I watched every minute and saw poverty like my own. Being poor in Canada sucks. Being poor and Indigenous from the Rez sucks. But being poor, and Indigenous, and disconnected from your identity in the city sucks too. The holes in Frank's home were like mine, the home without any food was familiar, the absent father was similar, and that poor mother carrying it all was too familiar.

What a fucking story!

If he could get through that shit, I could. I couldn't get Andrew Bennett's Irish accent out of my head, so I watched the movie again and again. I showed it to my brother and my friends. My mom cried as we watched. I bought the book and read it. Each line was filled with warm rhythmic intonations. When I read the last line, "'Tis," I was changed. The story had changed my mind about reading and planted a seed about education that festered within me. He loved school. It was his salvation. Could it be mine?

I wanted to know what happened next, so I picked up Frank McCourt's second book, 'Tis, and saw the struggle of a young immigrant in New York and his time in undergraduate university. While I was reading, I was applying to the University of Alberta's transfer year program for Indigenous kids. I wanted to become the teacher I wished I'd had, so those kids might never have to feel the same feelings that I experienced. I wanted to make school their escape and show them that the tools of empowerment were within the very institution that had oppressed us for generations.

I was forced to read all over again. My funding required me to take an Indigenous literature course and I discovered a plethora of stories like Angela's Ashes, but even better. Their vulnerability mirrored my own. My very life was on the pages. The stories by these amazing Indigenous authors danced in my mind. I fell in love with Richard Van Camp, Eden Robinson, Thomas King, Louise Erdrich, Rita Joe, and Drew Hayden Taylor.

By the time I got around to reading McCourt's third book, Teacher Man, I was teaching on the Enoch reserve and helping build a high school. I spent all my time convincing kids that getting an education mattered. I started telling stories, like McCourt does, about my past and connecting those stories to Alberta's educational outcomes. I showed those kids all the wonderful narratives from our own people that I had learned in undergrad, and, of course, I sprinkled in some Frank McCourt. I was deep inside the institution I once hated, and I felt a bit dirty, like I had become the assimilated NDN that Thomas Scott wanted. It was bittersweet, because I also found freedom and an escape from poverty.

I continued to tell stories. Students always asked for more, and, for the longest time, I thought they just wanted to avoid doing work. I mean, it was exactly what I would have done if I'd had a teacher who told stories. My mentor and good friend Dr. Dale Ripley thought it was valuable to have a high school teacher on the Rez who was an Indigenous high school dropout. Ripley felt my story could help

Indigenous kids. When I transferred from that Rez to a "regular" school division, the students there also loved the stories about my life.

There was a part of me that felt like simply having an undergraduate degree wasn't good enough to show that I had made it. Something in me needed more proof that I wasn't the kid who was in Mr. Indifferent's class. Graduate school felt different than undergrad. I didn't struggle; I thrived. Being Indigenous wasn't a burden; it was sexy. I quickly discovered that I was an extremely rare teacher — special in a different way. Maybe, I was Mr. Inadifferentway. How many of me are out there: an inner city Indigenous high school dropout who got a teaching degree, helped build a high school on the Rez, and taught in "regular" Canadian schools? Seemed rare enough — and my professors felt the same, so I started writing about my own experiences with education. I pretended to be an Indian Frank McCourt, and the University of Alberta was thirsty for Indigenous stories.

Something magical happened. I got As — lots of them. I got positive reinforcement — lots of it. I got endless encouragement and demand for the stories of my life. It was wonderful and an easy way to get through graduate school.

But it was more than that.

The stories changed my life because they landed on the eyes of Dr. Jean Clandinin, who encouraged me to apply for this brand-new program called Audible's Indigenous Writer's Circle. Apparently, Audible was looking for Canada's next Indigenous author, and she insisted that I was that person. So I did, and they loved it.

Audible assigned me Chelsea Vowel as a mentor and she encouraged me to turn my stories into a memoir. So I did, just like Frank McCourt did. I called it *Concrete NDN*. When the memoir found its way to Richard Van Camp, he agreed to copy edit it for me. It felt surreal to have him love my stories as much as I loved his. When he finished, we exchanged stories for hours, and we discussed how our stories help our people. He stood on his porch yelling at me, "It's an incredible memoir and it is going to get published! Faith and trust my brother! Faith and trust!" I felt warm and fuzzy having created something that could help others the way McCourt's books helped me.

Richard encouraged me to write more. That felt right. I decided to apply to UBC's MFA for Creative Writing, and with the help of Richard and Chelsea, I recently accepted their offer.

But I'll tell you this. If I ever run into Mr. Indifferent again, he still isn't getting that report.

Unquiet Slumbers

ILEANA GONZÁLEZ ZAVALA

The intense horror of nightmare came over me; I tried to draw back my arm,
but the hand clung to it, and a most melancholy voice sobbed,
"Let me in—let me in!"

(*Wuthering Heights* by Emily Brontë)

Why would he not let me in, this strange man, this outsider who clearly doesn't belong here? I wailed and wailed, begged to be let in, back in my home, to my life, but he would not yield. How odd! Does he know who I am? Doesn't he realize I am the lady of the house? Doesn't he know my name?

My name. But what is my name? I can hardly remember, so much did it change, so long ago it was. Why did I say Linton? Were the other names less important? And yet, it is the last name I remember, when I was lying in the midst of all these faces shouting at me, calling me back, and all I could hear was a distant cry, the wail like a forgotten newborn child's.

But still he would not let me in. I thought he had called for me. Did he not say my names from long ago? Did he not trace and mumble through the long-forgotten, faded writing on the ledge? *Catherine Earnshaw, Catherine Heathcliff, Catherine Linton*, over and over in a place that once belonged to only me?

A place that once belonged to me. I never thought I'd be so tied down to a place, but leaving permanently changes things. When we arrived in Canada from Mexico in late August, it felt to us like winter rather than summer. The leaves were yellow, orange, hectic red, and the wind had a cold bite that went all the way to our bones. The land was rather plain, with no hills in sight, let alone mountains. Even the smell was different, fishy, as if coming straight from the surrounding lakes. My name was not the same in this odd language, where words are not always pronounced how you'd expect. Names and places, pieces of who we are. The haunting began.

★ ★ ★

No wonder I can't remember my name. It always seemed to change, and now I can't decide which one was right. Perhaps they all were, or perhaps it doesn't matter much. Twenty years have passed, twenty years of solitude and oblivion, and me, wandering alone in the moors, trying to find my way home, calling for him until my voice becomes doleful—what has become of me? Why can I not come home? Why won't he let me in?

It's twenty years, twenty years. I've been a waif for twenty years!

I had lost my way. I could see the heights from my bedroom window, far in the distance, shining bright like a refuge in the middle of a tempest. They're waiting for me at the house, of course they are, and I must go home. I must go home.

———————

The girl from a year ago, with the heavy black eyeliner and the long curly hair, dressed in a constant rotation of old t-shirts and jeans and black Converse, couldn't quite make it over here. Instead, she slowly disappeared. She became someone else, someone she didn't know. Dislocated and alone, the spectral girl had to retreat, to hide and wander until found again.

★ ★ ★

How did I become so lost? We knew the moors so well, all our lives wandering through them, hiding from the world, from my irascible brother, from that self-righteous old man, from the life we thought we could escape. It seemed possible there, in the desolate moors. We felt so alive; we thought we belonged. If I could find him, he would lead me home. He called and called for me to come back. Why is he not here? Why does he not come back for me?

But even now I hear him calling, sobbing as much as I did when that horrible stranger would not let me in. He bids me enter and calls me his heart's darling. He begs me to return and to hear him this time. But I do hear him. I have come back, just as he desires, inescapably drawn to his frantic cries, pulled back by his desperate words. Can he not feel me here, outside the window? Can he not hear me, wailing in this stormy wind, asking to be let back in?

———————————

Sometimes I could feel her asking to be let back in, but it was hard to remember her after all those years, that girl who was me, a peeking shadow, an echo. I began to collect books. Different colours and sizes, multiple editions of the same novels I had read year after year. The friends I grew up with had changed and become people I didn't know, but the books didn't change. I returned to them. In that space of recollection, a phrase or sentence would pull back the old ghost and bid it come, until unaware, as the years went by, the girl haunted me again.

★ ★ ★

I thought he wished to be near me again. I heard him long ago, cursing my name. Or was it a blessing? I couldn't tell. And yet he said he wanted me here with him. He prayed for me to come back, to be with him always, not to leave him in this abyss, to haunt him. He said he could not live without his life, without his soul. I thought he wanted to be with me always. Why can he not see that I am here, that I never left, that I could not leave? We are one, he and I. Surely he knows that he is always, always in my mind as my own being, that I am him. I try to call for him, but he will not hear me. How odd. I thought he wished it.

Catherine Earnshaw, may you not rest, as long as I am living! You said I killed you—haunt me, then! The murdered do haunt their murderers. I believe—I know that ghosts have wandered on earth. Be with me always—take any form—drive me mad! Only do not leave me in this abyss, where I cannot find you!

He was standing by the fireplace, silent, with his back towards me. I fancied that his tall, broad figure was shaking as he determinedly refused to face me. I could not understand why, after all this time, after our separation, after the end that awaited me, he would not come to me. I watched him jealously, suspiciously, his every movement waking a new sentiment in me. I couldn't stop gazing at him, thinking of all that had passed between us, of the past we shared together, of the unattainable future, of the horrible things he'd done and would continue to do.

How had we come to this? And he would not even look at me. I thought he wanted me. I thought all he wanted was to be with me again, now, and forever. Because our souls are one. Because we're the same being. And yet he would not come to me. Would he not relent a moment to keep me out of the grave? And yet he will not come near me. Ah, so that is how I'm loved! Well, never mind. That is not my Heathcliff. I shall love mine yet; and take him with me—he's in my soul.

I wonder he won't be near me! I thought he wished it. Heathcliff, dear! you should not be sullen now. Do come to me, Heathcliff!

Sometimes I think he hears me, sees me, knows that I'm with him in the very rooms we haunted as children. He leans against the ledge of an open lattice and looks not outside, but towards the room, earnestly trying to catch a glimpse of something, but he does not seem to see me, standing right there. He looks different now, his face gaunter and paler, his black hair less lustrous, his dark eyes fiercer than ever. He has changed, ever so slightly, from the sobbing man standing by my fireplace, refusing to show me his face. He has changed, but why? It has not been long since I saw him that fateful day in Thrushcross Grange. How long ago? Twenty years, for twenty years I've been a waif. I did not think it had been so long, and me alone, wandering forever, lost on the moors.

Years pass, and the new place is not new anymore. When we drive through the country, passing field after field full with new crops, with the scattered farmhouses and barns, and lonely trees popping here and there, I can see the beauty in this flat land. When I walk through the parks and trails, with their luscious woods and trees and burbling creeks, life here is tangible and quick. Faces that were once new have become well-known and loved. The cold winds don't feel as cutting, even if the winters are still long. The sunless winters make my skin paler, and white hair weaves itself on my dark curls. And the ghost? She doesn't show herself too often, but when she does, it's almost like an old friend coming to visit.

★ ★ ★

I think he sees me. I stand in front of him and he looks right at me. He smiles and does not remove his glittering, restless black eyes. There's a woman with him, an old woman, telling him to eat and drink. Is it Nelly? How can Nelly look so old? She seems scared of something, perhaps of Heathcliff. He asks her if they are by themselves. She thinks he is talking nonsense, yet she looks about the room to check, as if caught in a superstitious trance, while Heathcliff stretches out his hand in the space before him, close to where I stand. Finally, after these long years, after all this wandering, he knows I'm here.

Sometimes we walk on the moors again, as we did when we were children, hiding from the world. There is no one after us now—no one wishes to come near. Sometimes we see people in the distance, and we think they can also see us, but they quickly move away, as if terrified. We don't care; we are together at last. One soul, one being, forever on our beloved moors, where we always belonged. Let no one imagine we have unquiet slumbers, for we have returned home.

The ghosts never leave. They wander, haunted and haunting, unseen by common eyes. But sometimes, in an unexpected moment, in a transitory look, they are revealed. A quick look in a mirror shows a glimpse of dark, almond-shaped eyes, darkened further by the black kohl that fully encircles them, piercing with an intensity that says, let me in, let me in. She comes back to me from fifteen years ago, but only for a moment, and I let her in. When a specific song plays, when I smudge my black eyeliner, when I read the story of Catherine and Heathcliff for what feels like the hundredth time, her ghost reappears. The haunting can feel like coming home. She'll be here for a moment, and then quietly slip away, until the next time a spark brings her back to haunt the self I have become. After many wanderings, many years of haunting, I cannot imagine she has unquiet slumbers, for she has returned home.

Resistance Written in Blood

HEATHER MCCARDELL

Afterwards we stood on a little bridge and looked at the huge goldfish — more dull and white than gold. "Ugh," he said. "They look like blood-soaked bandages." I thought he was pretentious. "What d'you know of blood-soaked bandages?" I asked and spoiled his poetry.

(*Mrs. Blood* by Audrey Thomas)

Growing up, my period was a source of shame. My parents would tell me, in low voices, "Wrap your pads a bit tighter or put them in the downstairs bathroom. They're a little smelly," and girls at school would whisper to each other, "Does anyone have a tampon?" We would ask our friends to check our bottoms discreetly to make sure redness hadn't leaked through our denim, and teachers would give us a hard time about going to the bathroom — "You should have gone during your lunch break or between classes" — so we either had to admit we had our period in front of the whole class, which was absolutely mortifying, or sit for fifty minutes and hope we'd packed a sweater to tie around our waist later. As grateful as I am for the supportive community of schoolgirls who always had each other's backs, situations like these cloak menstruation in deep shame and continue to make it — and, consequently, one's body — feel dirty, wrong, and far from normal.

An additional "far from normal" feeling occurred when my period refused to become regular. While my friends complained about their monthly bleeds or said things like "I can't go to the beach that week. That's when I'm supposed to get my period," I lit up with anxiety at the fact that I didn't have a set monthly schedule — that I could go to the beach and, *of course*, that's when my irregular period would arrive. I spent most of my middle school years wearing pads or panty liners every day, fearing it would show up unexpectedly and then racing desperately to wrench my pants down in the safety of a bathroom stall to find — nothing. No sign of red or brown streaks, splotches, or clots. Not even a smudge. Just the white cottony fabric looking the same as it had when I'd torn it from its wrapping that morning. So not only did I have a period, a supposedly taboo, wrong, and shameful thing, but mine also refused to cooperate with its promised regularity, making it especially taboo, decidedly wrong, and particularly shameful.

Only a handful of people in my life knew about the uterine-ripping, breast-aching, pimple-popping horror that graced me with its presence every three to four months. When girls at school passed around tampons and pads, muttering that they *once again* had their periods, I joined in, agreeing about this annoying monthly bleeding to conceal that I was a fake, an imposter, a fraud. Sure, I had a period, but it only came three to four times a year. Did it even count? My unreliable menstruation disgraced me, so I kept it secret.

Flash forward seven years: I'd made it through high school and had only a year left of my undergrad. Hormonal birth control had regulated my irregularity for most of that time. One day, I thought to myself, "I wonder if I'd be regular by now if not for the pill." Was I finally normal? I contacted my doctor, who said, "Sure. It's been a few years. Let's see if your body has righted itself." So, I went off the hormones and waited.

One month went by. *She said it would be normal to miss the first month.*

Two months went by. *Maybe my body is still regulating itself. Getting used to things?*

Three months went by. *She said wait for four.*

Four months went by. *Where did I put her number?*

I didn't get a natural period for nine whole months. (I know what you're thinking, and no, I wasn't.) What was originally abnormal was now *especially* abnormal.

In the months that followed, I had ultrasounds, bloodwork, and a referral to an endocrinologist. The diagnosis: polycystic ovarian syndrome, or PCOS, something I would learn, years later, was much more common than anyone let on. Finally, I had unmasked the mystery of my irregular period.

In the spring of 2021, *Mrs. Blood* arrived in a cardboard box stuffed with textbooks for my MA in English Literature and Creative Writing. I read the book that June while completing my thesis, which involved researching and writing poetry on the mistreatment of women in the Canadian healthcare system. As I uncovered anecdotes and studies of how doctors and nurses dismiss women's health, I noticed that concerns to do with menstrual or reproductive health were especially ignored. So, I spent a lot of time that year thinking about bodies, including my own, and the silencing of "women's issues," like menstruation.

Now, *Mrs. Blood* isn't about periods, but it is about vaginal bleeding. In all my years of reading — for pleasure and for school — I hadn't ever read a book that depicted the leaking female body candidly, and not as uber magical or horrifyingly shameful. The protagonist, Mrs. Blood, experiences a miscarriage and subsequent bleeding. She revisits moments from her past as her sense of self shifts and fragments because of her infantilization by the nurses and doctors in the hospital (and yes, I did write my final paper for that summer course on exactly this topic). Thomas writes the miscarriage without metaphors, which tend to evoke secrecy and detach the process from the body. Instead, she details in plain language the "sticky ooze of blood between my legs" and the placenta ripping from the uterine wall in agonizing spasms. Graphic, I know, but also amazing in the realistic depictions of bodily processes. That is what *Mrs. Blood* gave to me: the beginnings of my own resistance to a patriarchal culture that understands my body as wrong, and the realization that women have been writing about their bodies as forms of resistance for decades.

Here, I'm reminded of the language we used as girls to talk about our periods amongst ourselves. We always had code names: Aunt

Flow, Shark Week, time of the month. My childhood best friend and I called it our "peach" for extra secrecy. We were always afraid someone who wasn't supposed to hear — a boy, a brother, a dad — would catch on. We relied on these codes, needed them even. But not Audrey Thomas, and not *Mrs. Blood*. Theirs was a lexicon of full-on bleeding, blood, and clots.

Mrs. Blood undercuts patriarchal control and brings autonomy to women's bodies, specifically to unmentionable functions like menstruation and miscarriage. The importance, to me, is Thomas's choice to write unapologetically about an aspect of bodies that girls and women have learned to hide. To all that secrecy, Thomas says *No!*

Reading this book helped me work through some of my pre-existing anguish about my body and its especially taboo, decidedly wrong, and particularly shameful irregular periods. It gave me *resistance* — against a patriarchal culture that tells me my vaginal bleeding is shameful, against my own belief that my body wasn't normal, and against people who tell girls and women to keep these things to themselves. In terms of my relationship with my body, this book gave me some acceptance. I no longer feel abnormal or disgraceful. And clearly, vaginal bleeding is a hot topic, one that has spanned decades and generations. *Mrs. Blood* is a book older than me; people wanted to read it — are *still* reading it — and I am a member of this community.

Back in my middle school and high school years, we'd talk about our periods in the bathroom, pausing when we heard voices of passing students or teachers outside, and resuming once they'd gone; we'd talk about our periods in the locker room as we changed for gym, confiding in each other that today we'd fake cramps to get out of playing soccer or volleyball; we'd talk about our periods out on the field during the lunch break, how walking supposedly eased the pain, but "I can still feel it!" In these spaces, our voices were never hushed, never whispered. We'd talk loudly, strongly, sometimes yell over the wind. In these spaces, we felt safe. Not embarrassed. Not abnormal. Not shameful. *Mrs. Blood* made me feel as though I was back in those safe spaces, and I hope that one day all menstruating individuals can feel that safety, both inside and outside of a book.

You are Dust

EMILY TABOREK

So she departed, she and her companions, and bewailed her virginity on the mountains. At the end of two months, she returned to her father, who did with her according to the vow he had made.

(*The Bible, NRSVCE*)

Raped. Murdered. Traded. Sold. Leaf through the pages of the Bible and this is what you find. These are the fates of our ancestors. I still remember when I first read of Jephthah's triumphant victory. My grandfather's Jerusalem Bible lay open to the last pages of Judges. The gilded leaves were static, saturated with blood. Not a page fluttered with the sigh of a girl's last breath. The last words of the book of Judges stayed with me: "In those days there was no king in Israel. Everyone did what was right in his own eyes." In his own eyes. Not hers, but his. Oh sweet, unnamed daughter of Jephthah, who went quietly to her death for her father's victory, you deserved so much better. When you heard that he traded your life for a simple battle, you submitted to him. You asked for just one thing: to go to the mountains to bewail your virginity. Dear Bat-Jephthah, even in death, your only regret was that you did not please a man with your body, or bear his children, and grow his seed. It is said that every year, the women go into the mountains to mourn you, dear sister, but they do not. You are forgotten, beloved. You are dust.

You are the dust that rose behind the Levite as he rode on his donkey from Gibeah to the hill country of Ephraim. You watched as he cut his wife into pieces — reader, don't you dare call her his concubine — and sent each piece throughout Israel. You are the dust of the armies marching to assault the Benjamanites to feed the ego of one man, to slaughter thousands, to rape and kidnap the women and children. You silently cheered as the Levite's wife did what you could not: she attempted to take her life into her own hands; she left her husband to live with her father. You stood by as she was thrown to the wolves and used as the catalyst to more violence. Alas, you are dust. You could only watch.

You are the dust Tamar put on her head as she tore her robe and wailed aloud. She was like you, Bat-Jephthah: the dutiful daughter. She was prudent and knowledgeable of the laws of Israel and acted to protect her brother in his crimes against her. She and you are sisters, ground to dust under the heel and savage weight of fathers and brothers you are too obedient to resist. In your time, Bat-Jephthah, there was no king in Israel. In her time there was only her father. Was her fate all that different from yours? You are the dust that lies on the empty seat of justice.

You are the dust that packs itself in a neat layer on a large tome in St Peter's Seminary library. I brush the dust off the cover and crack the spine — unopened. I hold in my hands the book I've been looking for to complete my essay on Judith, just one of the hundreds of books I've rooted out of the Seminary library. This one sounds like a slog: *Women in Scripture: A Dictionary of Named and Unnamed Women in the Hebrew Bible, the Apocryphal and Deuterocanonical Books, and the New Testament.* A dictionary? How exciting. I take it over to one of the tables in the always-empty reading room, waving to the statue of St. Francis de Sales on my way.

Inside the book, I found my life. I discovered my ancestors. I found unspeakable horror, unbelievable strength, freedom and femininity, suffering and subjugation, all within the short entries of the encyclopedia. Inside the book, there were stories of biblical women, neatly organized in alphabetical entries. Hello, Abigail 1, wife of Nabal.

Abigail 2, sister of David, nice to meet you. And so it went, down and down and down, from Abi to Zosara. The book does not end with the last Z name, but continues onto an even larger section: "Unnamed Women". The entries take on different names now: "Blemished Women," "Woman Caused to Miscarry," "Girls as Booty," "Barren Women," "Virgin," "Prostitute," "Adulteress."

Below each name is described a woman. These are the women of my history. The most obscure women in the Bible, forgotten even by scholars, are placed on a pedestal of their own. The sun went down unnoticed through the ornate windows of the Seminary reading room while I met my mothers, sisters, and aunts.

Dearest Bat-Jephthah, you watched as I rediscovered you.

I inhaled the book front to end, thumbing through my grandfather's Bible as I went, its gilded pages barely resembling brass by the time I was through. The book rewrote the Bible in my mind. The old family Bible shone with a new light in my eyes and, as a new woman, I now viewed it. This moment marked the beginning of my fascination — obsession? — with Biblical women and the field of Biblical studies. The unassuming encyclopedia led me to Alice Ogden Bellis's *Helpmates, Harlots, and Heroes*. That small, colourful book incited a personal revolution. Before reading her book, I considered myself somewhat analytical when it came to the Bible. Now, I see how ignorant I was. Soon after, every woman in my Roman Catholic family was deconstructing patriarchal narratives and rewriting the story of Lot's daughters.

I was ravenous for more, needed more. I changed majors at university, interrogated professors, shouted until I was accepted to learn at a seminary. Once there, the triumph faded, and I realized I was an outcast. Only nineteen, I looked with leery eyes at the rows of older men that made up my class. Those men were not to blame, no, of course not, but the wounds of women past still pulsed under my skin as I learned of Church Fathers and Popes and Patriarchs, and of the boys' club of Catholicism that I try to see has changed.

The men in my class, prospective priests, were the cream of the crop. They were smart, respectful, merciful, and loud. In their sweeping generalizations about the state of the Church, the state of society, and the state of men, they spoke on behalf of humanity without a second thought. I stood to the side and watched. Who was I to intrude on their sacred brotherhood? Who was I to insert my feminine narrative, my experiences and insight, into their masculine monarchy? I sat still and silent for so long that I became dust.

Throughout it all, I returned to my Bible. The voices locked inside the treasured tome continued to cry out to me. I swore I would never allow them to be buried again as they had been throughout the ages. Each year since the first pen blackened the first page, they have been buried under fistfuls of dirt thrown by triumphant hands, then stamped under triumphant heels. I vowed to face the mud and the men, break fingernails and relationships until I had dug out their storied faces and put them on display.

Yet, they do not belong on display. For millennia, these women have been in Bibles and paintings, strung up for all to see, raped over and over in discussions and parables, trapped in a never-ending horror story, never to rest. I wish to give them rest, to celebrate these women's lives and share their untold strengths and successes, not to dwell on their deaths, rapes, and humiliations.

Go tell it on the mountain: these women acted with cunning and bravery when all the black print tells is how they were used as tools of men.

Go shout it from the rooftop: the women the black print depicts as vile and wicked were acting for their survival in a world designed for their subjugation.

Go scream it from the cliffside: for thousands of years, these sordid stories in black print were used to cow, bully, and beat women into inferiority based on the abuses of their ancestors.

Go, speak softly, and make a change.

The change cannot be in the black print — the time for changing the Bible has long since passed. The change must take place in the hearts and minds of the people. Please, reader, teach your daughters about the strength and cunning Tamar displayed when exacting her rights from Judah. Tell them of the incredible bravery of Jael and

Judith. Warn them of how the most revered figures in the holiest of books treated the women closest to them: how Abraham sacrificed Sarah's dignity and risked her life in Egypt to protect his own, how Isaac disowned Rebekah out of fear, and how Lot offered his daughters to rapists. Teach your daughters to discover their history and to celebrate their ancestors. And reader, please tell your sons. Tell your brothers, fathers, uncles. This is not — *cannot* — just be a women's issue. This is a human issue. Give everyone you know the tools to see the Bible in a new light, and if they can't see it, tell them the stories. Tell their stories and create change in the world. Do not let these women lie in oblivion.

I will tell their stories.

I will tell mine.

Together, we will no longer be dust.